PRAISE FOR HOW TO PHYSICALLY DEVELOP AN ELITE SOCCER PLAYER

"Matteo and Jeff are excellent practitioners who have developed their skills working with some of the most talented young football players in the country. This book will be a superb resource for those wishing to develop the physical qualities of future players whether that be grass roots or elite."

Mark Armitage, English FA Consultant

"Matteo and Jeff have provided a fantastic resource for training young footballers with this book. I myself have undertaken drills and exercises from the book, which helped me to optimise my physical development and make it to the elite level"

Jake Hesketh, Southampton FC Footballer

"Jeff and Matteo have succeeded in providing a very thorough yet simple and concise reference for those involved in the development of young soccer players. Whilst it is crucial for young players to be exposed to the right training stimulus at the right time in their development, it is also crucial for a fun and stimulating environment to ensure the love of 'playing' the game remains paramount. The drills and exercises shown in the book will certainly help achieve this balance."

Nick Harvey, English FA Physical Performance Coach

"This is an excellent text for those looking to gain a better understanding of physical development and its implications in youth football. The information, examples, and guidance provided in this book are based upon sound scientific principles and ideal for the coach working with the developing athlete."

Dr Sean Cumming, Lead Scientist in Premier League Growth Study
& Senior Lecturer for Sport and Exercise Science at the University of Bath

HOW TO PHYSICALLY DEVELOP AN ELITE SOCCER PLAYER: AGES 8-16

MATTEO CONTI AND JEFF LEWIS

The Book Guild Ltd

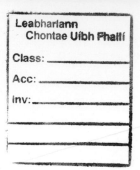
First published in Great Britain in 2016 by
The Book Guild Ltd
9 Priory Business Park
Wistow Road, Kibworth
Leicestershire, LE8 0RX
Freephone: 0800 999 2982
www.bookguild.co.uk
Email: info@bookguild.co.uk
Twitter: @bookguild

Typeset in Aldine401 BT

Printed and bound in Great Britain by CPI Group (UK) Ltd, Croydon, CR0 4YY

ISBN 978 1911320 098

British Library Cataloguing in Publication Data.
A catalogue record for this book is available from the British Library.

MIX
Paper from
responsible sources
FSC® C013604
FSC
www.fsc.org

CONTENTS

INTRODUCTION

The participation and importance of youth soccer worldwide is continually growing as the demand and finances within the game increase, with more and more young players seeking that professional contract at 16 years of age. In order to reach that coveted contract a player is required to possess a high level of technical, tactical and physical qualities. With the speed and intensity of the game constantly increasing the need to develop quicker, stronger and more powerful soccer players is a necessity for success.

Developing these key physical qualities requires a long term, multifaceted plan. Long Term Athlete Development (LTAD) is a framework used by many soccer and sporting organisations in order to develop the physical piece of the jigsaw in young players. The complexity of this pathway has further increased in the 21st century with the expansion of sports science, and as a result many coaches may miss key points or get lost in scientific jargon when attempting to develop a pathway for their young players.

We provide a comprehensive explanation of the key topics associated with developing those physical qualities within soccer, using scientifically backed research as well as drawing on our own experience from working within the elite academy system. By the end of the book you will be able to follow a step by step logical and progressive physical development pathway with age specific games and exercises for you to deliver to your players. We feel that our long term plan will prepare a young player for the physical demands that are required from soccer, and place them in an excellent position of getting the coveted professional contract.

GROWTH AND MATURATION

When discussing the physical development of young soccer players it is important to understand maturation, and the key role it plays.

It is first important to identify the difference between growth and maturation. Growth refers to 'measurable changes in size, physique, body composition, and various systems of the body' (Malina et al., 2004). Maturation is defined as 'the timing and tempo of progress towards the mature state' (Malina et al., 2004). The timing and tempo of maturation considerably varies between individuals (Malina et al., 2004), and such variation in progress over time implies a variation in the rate of change. Growth therefore continues throughout an individual's life; however, maturation comes to an end when an individual has reached the mature state.

Maturation is important within youth soccer as it can result in substantial differences between children. Individuals could be of the same size but they can vary at the point they are on in their path to adult size or maturation (Malina et al., 2004). It is therefore important that the players within your squads are treated as individuals rather than equally, with the training environment matching their biological rather than chronological age. This may require a player being moved up an age, down an age or performing a modified training session. Coaching in this way will ensure they are always testing and developing their technical ability.

Within the general population, boys advanced in maturity status have been found to be taller and heavier (Malina et al., 2004). The hormone activity associated with puberty is the primary cause of height and weight gains, and therefore height and weight are strongly linked to pubertal status (Malina et al., 2004). A large portion of this increase in weight is accounted for by increases in muscle mass, with measures of muscularity showing early maturing boys to have significantly greater muscle mass than late maturing boys (Roemmich and Rogol, 1995). These differences have also been shown to exist within youth soccer populations (Malina et al.,2000; Malina et al., 2005; Figueiredo et al., 2010; Carling et al., 2012), however the differences in height, weight and muscle mass between early and later maturing boys is not found to continue into adulthood (Pearson et al., 2006). Skeletally mature individuals within

1

a 15 – 16 age group were found to be shorter and heavier (Malina et al., 2000), a characteristic believed to be associated with their shorter growth period (Malina et al., 2004). Therefore at adulthood, the later maturing player is more likely to have a bigger stature due to their longer growth period.

Between the ages of 11 – 14 years, for boys, the effect of maturation has been found to vary most (Malina et al., 2005) as a result of differences in the timing and tempo of the adolescent growth spurt. The average age of the adolescent growth spurt, the timing of peak height velocity (PHV), is 13.8 years within boys (Malina et al., 2004). There has been less research exploring maturation within female soccer; however, the age of the adolescent growth spurt for a girl is around 12 years of age (Malina et al., 2004), with the greatest variation between the ages of 10 – 13 years.

Players are grouped by chronological age within soccer teams. As a result this can lead to maturity differences within the same age group being large, despite the relatively small (less than one year) differences in chronological age. An individual of early maturity status born at the start of the year can have a skeletal age more than four years in advance of an individual born at the end of the year who is of late maturity status, despite having a chronological age difference of eleven months (Malina et al., 2004).

The physical characteristic differences related to biological maturation have led to extensive research exploring biological maturation and its effects on physical performance tests. Research has found early maturing soccer players to possess greater speed, strength and power during the adolescent years (Malina et al., 2004; Vaeyens et al., 2006; Figueiredo et al., 2010; Carling et al., 2012). This physical advantage has also been confirmed within match play. Global Positioning System (GPS) has been used to show players of more advanced maturity status to have greater locomotion and running performance within U15 youth soccer matches (Buchheit and Mendez-Villanueva, 2014). The physical characteristic differences relating to biological maturation within youth female populations is far less clear and has received less attention within research. Increases in performance of strength, speed and power of early maturing girls are evident within literature (Beunen and Malina, 2007). However, the magnitude of this effect is less than in young boys. The physical advantage these early maturing players possess disappears once the players' reach adulthood as the later maturing players now are fully developed (Malina et al., 2004).

The physical advantages associated with early maturation influence talent identification protocol and team selection practice, with a greater percentage of squad players shown to be early in maturity status in comparison to the late maturity status (Figueiredo et al., 2009). This is combined with the relative age effect, in which a bias exists for players born in the earlier quarters of the selection year (Votteler and Höner, 2013). Selection practice of this nature prevents technically capable (or even superior) players developing to their full potential purely because they are of a later maturity status.

Several methods exist to assess the maturity status of young male and female soccer players.

These include the Khamis-Roche algorithm (Khamis and Roche, 1995) and the timing offset from PHV (Mirwald et al., 2002). These overcome the limitations associated with invasive methods of assessment (Leone and Comtois, 2007).

The identification of each player's maturity status within your squad provides you with valuable information. This information can be used to reduce the risk of injury, individualize training programs and enhance squad selection. When a player is going through their major growth spurt, PHV occurring at 92 % adult height (Sherar et al., 2005), they are at a greater risk of injury (Malina et al., 2004). Training load should be reduced appropriately during these periods. Training load can be reduced during phases of an individual's development when they are physically struggling by giving them less strenuous positions within training drills, or reducing training time. Twelve to eighteen months post-PHV there is a 'window of opportunity' whereby maximal gains in strength, speed and power can be developed. This is due to the increase in circulating hormones, such as testosterone, which allow for greater muscle mass development. Thus it is important to know the specific maturational time-points to capitalise on this 'window of opportunity' and individualise the training for each player. Maturity assessment can also be utilized to ensure players are in a soccer environment that matches their biological age rather than chronological age.

It is clear to see that maturation plays a pivotal role in the long term development of young soccer players. This book utilizes age based phases, but it is important for the coach to understand the individualization that is required within these phases.

FUNCTIONAL COMPETENCE

Good functional competency means that the body's movement system is working proficiently (Cook et al., 2014a), with adequate stability and mobility displayed when performing a functional movement, e.g. overhead squat. This competence base provides a solid foundation upon which functional capacity can be built. The importance of building strong functional competency is highlighted by its position at the base of the optimal performance pyramid (Cook, 2003).

If an individual displays good functional competency, positive adaptations will result from the training they perform (Cook et al., 2014a). However, in the presence of dysfunctional competency, such as mobility, stability and/or motor control issues, the same training stress has the potential to cause unnecessary injury risk (Cook et al., 2014a). Regardless of the equipment available or the program designed, performance improvements will not occur if functional competency issues are not exposed and improved through anatomical adaptation. The correct program design will ensure that each individual's functional weaknesses are fixed, by stretching tight areas and strengthening areas that are weak.

The assessment and monitoring of functional competency of young soccer players is therefore of great importance, and can be completed through screenings, such as the Functional Movement Screen (FMS) (Cook, 2003). These screening tests place an individual's body in extreme positions that require mobility and stability, whereby imbalances and areas of weakness can be identified. Literature has shown that a score of less than 14 out of 21 in the FMS shows a player is at greater risk of injury (Cook et al., 2014a), which instantly provides guidance as to who requires a great deal of mobility and stability work. The simplicity of the test does, however, mean that it does not offer the full insight into specific issues. A more thorough screen undertaken by a physiotherapist can pinpoint exact player weaknesses and make it easier to plan each player's individualized corrective program. The ability to get a physio assessment on all players is not an expense all teams can afford, and within these environments the more basic functional screens should be used.

Highlighting any functional competency issues and addressing these weaknesses is crucial, as completion of fundamental movements without correcting these functional competency issues will reinforce poor and inefficient movement patterns (Cook et al., 2014a). These inefficient and poor movement patterns lead to decrements in the physical performance of fundamental movements, but also an increased risk in the potential for injury to occur (Cook, 2011). The number one risk factor for future injury is previous injury history, after which the next biggest risk factor relates to a player's functional competence (Cook et al., 2014b). Motor control limitations in balance, stabilization and basic coordination, plus asymmetries like right to left imbalance in muscle activation and flexibility are all identified as injury risk factors (Cook et al., 2014a). Therefore, addressing these functional competency issues is of high importance to you, the coach.

Once these areas of weakness have been improved through corrective exercise programs, a player will be able to perform better movement within the gym (e.g. a squat) but more importantly on the pitch (e.g. a sprint).

Functional competence within young soccer players is, however, a complex process. Players in the pre-pubertal phase are likely to display excellent functional capacity (Blanksby et al., 1994) and the aim of the exercises these players perform will be to ensure that this functional competence remains. However, during the adolescent growth spurt, period of PHV, a player's functional competence is affected by their rapid growth (Malina et al., 2004). This period of development represents an important time in terms of functional competence, and players within this period should be regularly monitored and assessed through functional competency screens. Any areas identified as becoming weaknesses, should be addressed through individual corrective exercises. Adopting this approach will allow players to pass through their growth spurt maintaining an excellent functional competence base. This excellent functional base can then be built upon through training aimed at developing functional capacity. Functional competence should continue to be monitored and any weaknesses developed throughout the remainder of the player's career, as this will lead to continued enhancements in performance and reductions in the risk of injury.

The following exercises make up the index of functional competency exercises used within this book's physical development pathway.

EXERCISE INDEX:

o   Deadbug

The player should lie on their back with their arms straight in the air and their legs raised with a 90 degree bend at the knee. The player should then use their abdominal muscles to push their back flat against the floor. This represents the start position and they should then lower one leg while keeping everything else still. It should take a count of three to lower the leg and a count of three to raise the leg. The leg should be lowered until the heel touches the floor and the same knee angle should be maintained throughout the action. This represents one repetition and the player should then repeat with the other leg. It is important that the back remains pushed flat against the floor, to check this, the coach can try and put their hand under the player's lower back to see if an arch develops. If a player's back does not remain in contact with the floor throughout the drill, they should only lower their leg to the point where the back remains in contact with the floor.

Progression:
Now the player should straighten the leg on the way down rather than keeping it at 90 degrees.

o   Plank

On forearms and toes the player should lift their hips to a position where their body is a straight line. The head should be in neutral and they should suck in their belly button, thus activating their abdominal muscles. This position should then be held.

Progression:
The player should alternate in lifting a foot or arm (or both) off whilst maintaining body position. Also their arms or feet could be placed on an unstable surface (e.g. a swiss ball)

o   Side Plank

On one forearm and the side of one foot the player should lift their hips to a position where there is a straight line from their shoulder to their ankle. The head should be in neutral and they should activate their abdominal muscles by sucking in their belly button. This position should then be held. The exercise should then be repeated for the other side.

Progression:
The player should lift their free leg up to make a starfish shape. Further progress can be made by having the player on their hand rather than elbow.

o   Quadruped exercise

Starting with hands under shoulders and knees under hips, the player must maintain a straight back, and slowly lift one leg out behind until it is fully extended straight, then bring it back to start position. The exercise should be repeated for the other leg. The whole body should remain stationary with only the extending leg moving. The hips must not twist when the leg is extending.

Progression:

The player should now simultaneously lift the opposite arm during the movement, and then bring the leg and arm back to touch the opposite elbow with the leg at the start position.

This can be further progressed by having the player in a press up position when performing the same movement.

o   Oblique Crunch

The player should start with legs at 90 degrees and feet against the wall, sucking in their belly button and pushing their back flat against the floor. The player then brings their chin to their chest, and reaches across their body with the opposite arm. They must perform a pulsing action across their body while maintaining the body position; they should feel a burn down the side of their abdominals (i.e. in their obliques).

Glutes

o   Clams

The player should lie on their side, with their knees bent, and back in line with feet. They should brace their abdominal muscles and, without letting their hips fall back, open their legs while keeping their feet touching. They should then return to the start position and repeat. If the player's hips are falling back during the movement, hold their lower back up until they get used to the action.

Progression:
Place band around the player's knees.

o   Glute Bridge

The player should lie on their back, bend their knees and have their feet flat on the floor slightly closer then shoulder width apart. Bracing the core, they should push their back against the floor, then in a controlled manner lift their hips off the floor maintaining a stable spine. They should push through the heels of their feet and hold at the top position for a count of 3, before lowering and repeating.

Progression:
The player should place a band around their knees and push out against the band at the top of the bridge.

o   Single Leg Glute Bridge

The player should position themselves as they did for the glute bridge exercise. They should then extend one knee so that only one foot is in contact with the floor. Bracing the core, they should push their back against the floor, then in a controlled manner lift their hips off the floor. They should push through the heel of the foot on the floor to maintain a stable spine.

Progression:
At the top of the bridge the player should bring their opposite elbow and opposite knee together to touch and back again to the start position.

o   Band Walk

The player should place a band around their legs, just below the knee. They should lower to a quarter squat position. Maintaining this body position they should step to the side, leading with the knee. The trailing leg should follow, returning to shoulder width before the lead leg moves again.

Progression:

The player should increase the resistance of the band.

o   Clam Taps

The player should lie on their side, with their knees bent, and back in line with feet. They should brace their abdominal muscles and, without letting their hips fall back, open their legs. Bring their top foot in front of their shin; keeping the knee high they should perform taps with their heel to the floor as the leg moves up and down from the hip joint.

Proprioception

o   Single Leg Balance

The player should stand on one leg, with a slight bend in the knee and a slight bend in the hip (bum sticking out). This position should be maintained.

Progression:
o   Single Leg Balance eyes closed.
o   Single Leg Balance on disk (progress eyes closed).

Calf Mobility

o   Foam Roll

Using a foam roller, the player should roll from the top of the Achilles tendon to the bottom of the knee. The inside and outside of the calf should be rolled, concentrating on the sorest spots.

o   Calf Stretch 1

With arms shoulder width apart and one leg resting on top of the other, the player should continually stretch the leg straight, with heel pushed towards the floor.

o   Calf Stretch 2

The player should position their foot an inch away from a wall and push their knee towards the wall, maintaining their heel on the floor. The back leg should be in a relaxed position. If the heel lifts from the floor they need to move their front foot closer to the wall. If the knee touches the wall with their heel on the floor they should move their foot back to the furthest they can while maintaining a flat foot.

Hip Mobility

o   Foam Roll

Using a foam roller, the player should roll from the top of the knee tendon to the hip crease. The inside and outside of the quadriceps should be rolled, concentrating on the sorest spots.

o   Hip Flexor Stretch

The player should drop into a lunge position with one knee resting on the floor and lean forward into the stretch with their hips, with body remaining upright.

Progression:
The player should perform the hip flexor stretch with their back foot elevated.

FUNDAMENTAL MOVEMENT SKILLS

Fundamental movement skills are the basic motor activities that are the foundation for more complex sport specific activities (Wickstrom, 1983). Within soccer the fundamental movement skills would include running, jumping and changing direction. These movements will, however, be performed differently in soccer in comparison to other sports: for example, a soccer player will decelerate into the jockey position rather than the athletic position.

Combining good fundamental movement skills with good fundamental sport skills allows young soccer players to move more effectively and efficiently within a range of soccer situations (Higgs et al., 2008), ultimately enhancing the performance capabilities of the young soccer player. Without developing fundamental movement skills, to an adequate level, it will not be possible for a young soccer player to maximize their sport specific skills (Gallahue & Donnelly, 2007).

These fundamental movement skills are built upon good functional competency, (again highlighting the importance of building a good base), and progressed through initially closed training drills. A closed drill is one in which there is no form of reaction and the movement is preplanned, allowing the player to focus on the movement itself (Jeffreys, 2012). In an open drill the player has to react to stimuli which can become progressively more soccer specific (Jeffreys, 2012). These closed drills educate the correct movement patterns before the player is tested in an open manner. The drills within each phase of this book follow this progression, initially teaching the player the correct movement pattern in a closed drill before testing it in an open drill, replicating the unpredictable nature of a soccer match.

Like functional competency, basic fundamental movement skills are initially taught to players within the first phase of development. The age of the players within this phase means that the drills will be fun, and completed in an environment to match the concentration skills and energy levels of these players. These sport specific fundamental movement skills will then become more soccer specific as the player progresses through the future phases.

The development of fundamental movement skills is also affected by the periods of major growth that occur during adolescence (Malina et al., 2004). During a young soccer player's PHV, they are likely to experience reductions in their coordination as a result of the rapid growth in limb length, known as adolescence awkwardness (Malina et al., 2004). This reduction in coordination can affect an individual's ability to perform fundamental movement skills, as well as sport specific skills (Malina et al., 2004), resulting in the potential for temporary losses in speed, power and strength (Philippaerts et al., 2006). Throughout this period it is important to monitor and manipulate a player's training to ensure that reinforcement of the correct fundamental movement skills is completed. Regression during this period may be progression for an individual who is struggling. Once through this period of rapid growth the player can build their functional capacity upon these excellent movement skills. The maximal gains in muscle size and strength during the 'window of opportunity' can lead to large gains in speed and power output if the appropriate functional capacity training is undertaken (Lloyd and Oliver, 2012).

Applying a long term approach to the physical development of fundamental movement skills has received attention in literature, with research citing this the most effective way to develop the physical ability of players (Bayli and Hamilton, 2004; Lloyd and Oliver, 2012). The development of fundamental movement skills within this book follows this long term strategy approved by scientific research.

The following index of techniques represents the key fundamental movement skills used within the physical development pathway discussed in this book.

INDEX OF TECHNIQUE

Acceleration

Acceleration requires two key technical points: an increase in body height and a progressive increase in step length. The player should increase their body height as shown above, and this can be emphasised by starting in a prone position (first picture on the right). The first five to ten metres of the player's sprint should involve a continually rising body height until they achieve an upright position as shown in the final picture above. The step length of the player should also increase during this phase. This technique ensures that the player is applying force horizontally to the ground while propelling themselves forwards.

Deceleration requires two technical points, a decrease in body height and a progressive decrease in step length. The player should decrease their body height as shown above (from first picture on the right to last picture on the left), finishing in the athletic position shown in the final picture. The step length of the player should also decrease during this phase. The distance taken to decelerate will become progressively smaller with training. This technique ensures that the player is maintaining a body position that will allow them to change direction quickly.

Half Turn Body Shape

Right half turn (direct opponent to the right)   *Left half turn (direct opponent to the left)*

In soccer a player will not decelerate into an athletic position, as this square position makes it easier for an opponent to take the ball past them. To take control of defending an opponent the player should decelerate into the half turn 'jockey' position. The half turn position requires the player to have their weight evenly distributed between feet, their hips and chest forwards and their feet at roughly a 45 degree angle. This technique allows the player to dictate the direction the opponent goes. This technique also allows the player to easily turn backwards if a player tries to go past them, but also allows them to quickly accelerate forwards if they need to press.

Back Foot Pivot

In soccer the attacking opponent is unlikely to willingly let the defender dictate the direction they go. As a result they will often try to get past the defender by moving from side to side. It is therefore important that the defensive player is able to respond, and to do so they need to perform a pivot. This pivot is completed on their back foot and will result in their body position changing from the left half turn position to the right half turn position, as shown in the pictures above. Body shape should remain forwards throughout.

Change of Direction

| Backward Acceleration | Forward Acceleration | Lateral Acceleratiom |

To change direction the player requires an initial lowering of their body height. They then accelerate using the same technical points discussed in the acceleration section above. The other key technical aspect is the foot that makes the first step. When accelerating backwards from the half turn position the player makes a small first step using their front foot, whipping their knee around their body. When accelerating forwards from the jockey position they require the back foot to make a small first step. When accelerating laterally the outside leg makes the first small step, again whipping the knee around the body.

Jumping and Landing

Jumping is initiated by a small triple flexion of the ankles, knees and hips. The hips sit backwards rather than forwards with the knees in line with the toes. The arms are simultaneously swung back behind the base of the body. This 'dip' is immediately followed by an explosive triple extension of the ankles, knees and hips, with the arms simultaneous swinging overhead, as shown in the picture above. The player then propels themselves into the air maintaining this straight body position, utilising their core muscles to maintain an upright trunk. On landing, the player performs a simultaneous triple flexion of the ankles, knees and hips, into a quarter squat. They make initial contact with the balls of their feet before transferring their weight to the back, ensuring that their knees are kept in line with their toes and do not collapse in, as well as keeping their head and trunk upright.

WEIGHT TRAINING

Weight training is an important component for overall conditioning and preparation to produce a physically able soccer player. Weight training has been shown to increase strength (Kraemer et al., 1989), jump height (Falk and Mor, 1996), sprint ability (Williams, 1991), and functional biomechanics (Hewett, Myer, and Ford, 2005). These physical assets directly impact performance. Weight training also plays a primary role in injury prevention (Faigenbaum et al., 2009) by strengthening the supporting structures, enhancing the ability of the muscles to absorb energy, and developing muscle balance around joints. There are also positive health and psycho-social benefits for youths in undertaking weight training programmes (Faigenbaum et al., 2009). Therefore, the use of weightlifting is essential for the young soccer player, and preparation for this starts from 8 years of age.

Functional competency is essential for weight training, because if a player cannot move through the full range in their joints then it is not safe to place more load on them. It is important, therefore, to have levels of progression when coaching a child how to lift. Initially, it should concentrate on how well they move, so this would be all body weight exercises in which you attempt to go through the full range of the movement and teach correct technique; then how well they move, along with how much they can lift, so progressively increasing the load in order to provide physiological adaptation, as long as it is performed safely and with correct technique. The exercises across all levels are technically the same but what is governed differently is the load and intensity.

It is important to have built the functional competency and technical proficiency by the time the player reaches their 'window of opportunity' this will allow for greater gains in strength, speed and power through increased loading in their weightlifting sessions. This will optimise their long term development.

The main exercises along with technique points and pictures are shown below. These exercises are then adapted throughout the course of the book in different age chapters for age appropriate development.

EXERCISE INDEX:

Squat

The player's feet should be slightly wider than shoulder width apart, turned out slightly, and then, with a controlled speed, the player should lower down with heels remaining on the floor, knees in line with toes, back straight and head up. Once the hip angle is lower than the knee angle, the player should accelerate back up to a standing position, driving through the heels whilst maintaining all above points.

Variations:
➢ Back Squat
➢ Front Squat
➢ Overhead Squat

Lunge

The player should step forward with one foot so feet are split, front foot flat and back foot on the balls of the feet. Throughout the course of the movement the front foot should remain flat. During descent, the player should bend the back leg, in order to not allow the front knee to drift forwards and go down till they are just above the ground. Back should be straight throughout with chest and head up, again driving through the heel of the front foot in order to return to starting position, then stepping forward with back foot.

Variations:
➢ Forward Lunge
➢ Backwards Lunge
➢ Sideways Lunge
➢ With Bar on Back or Overhead
➢ Holding Dumbbells in Hands

Deadlift

The player should have their feet shoulder width apart and slightly turned out, with flexion at the knees and hip. The hands should grip the bar at shoulder width. The back should be straight and the head in a neutral position. From the start position there should be an extension at the hip and knees, with the load moving into the player's heels. Throughout the lift the player's back should remain straight. At the top of the lift the player should fully extend the hips and have their shoulders back. The lift should be performed explosively; the training bar should then be returned to the floor with control, flexing at the knees and hips and maintaining a straight back.

The player should grip the bar at shoulder width. Knees should have a slight bend, now maintaining a straight back, they should lower the bar, down their legs hinging from the hip, until it is below their knees in a controlled manor. From this position they should extend at the hip, still maintaining the straight back position, back to the start position.

Variation:

> Single Leg Romanian Deadlift

The player should grip the bar slightly wider than shoulder width apart, with it resting across the front of their shoulders. Feet are hip width apart. The player should then perform a quick 'knee dip' followed by an explosive triple extension of the ankle, knee and hip, with a simultaneous shrug of the shoulders to drive the bar overhead. The bar should be caught over the crown of the head, and returned to the start position in a controlled manner.

Variation:

➤ Jerk – similar movement pattern with the feet now splitting into a lunge position when catching the bar overhead.

Snatch

The player should grip the bar with an overhand hook grip at a width such that the bar rests across the hip crease at the end of the second pull. At the start position, back should be flat, feet about shoulder width, feet slightly turned out to allow greater hip mobility, head up, and arms straight and locked. Keeping the same back angle to the floor the player should start lifting the bar off the floor by extending the knees and shifting their weight onto the heel of the foot. Once the bar passes the knees the player should then explosively triple extend and shrug the bar to generate enough momentum to lift high enough so they can drop under and catch it overhead. The player should be in an overhead squat position now and recover to standing by extending hips and knees.

Variations:

➤ Hang Snatch
➤ Snatch from Blocks

Clean

The player should grip the bar with an overhand hook grip at about shoulder width apart. At the start position the back should be flat, feet shoulder width and slightly turned out to allow greater hip mobility, head up, and arms straight and locked. Keeping the same back angle to the floor the player should start lifting the bar off the floor by extending the knees and shifting their weight onto the heel of the foot. Once the bar passes the knees the player should then explosively triple extend and shrug the bar to generate enough momentum to lift high enough so they can drop under and catch it in the front squat positon. The player should then recover to standing by extending hips and knees.

Variations:
➢ Hang Clean
➢ Clean from Blocks

When undertaking weight training it is essential that it is done so safely and with correct technique. We have provided you with the technical points. However, having a fully qualified strength and conditioning coach, especially when starting to load, is ideal in order to avoid risk of injury.

PLANNING AND PERIODISATION

For the physical development of young soccer players to be optimal it is important for the training to be appropriately planned and periodised. Planning refers to sessions being designed and prepared in advance (Beachle and Earle, 2008). Periodisation refers to the planned variation in training methods on a cyclic or periodic basis (Plisk and Stone, 2003). The goal of periodisation is to optimise physical development through exploiting training effects at optimal times, whilst managing fatigue, stagnation and preventing overtraining (Plisk and Stone, 2003). For this to be successful, planning and periodisation is a daily, weekly, monthly and seasonal process, and requires continual assessment. Throughout the phases of this book it is important for the coach to plan and periodise the sessions appropriately, with the level of detail progressing as the players get older. Failure to correctly plan and periodise a player's development will prevent them from reaching their physical potential (Lloyd and Oliver, 2013).

Correct periodisation will provide players with the gradual overload that ensures they continue to develop physically. To create this overload the body needs to be stressed (Beachle and Earle, 2008). This overload can be in the form of an exercise becoming more advanced, during earlier phases where functional capacity is not a focus, or overloaded during later phases through more reps, sets and resistance of an exercise being performed. This later stress causes damage to the body (Beachle and Earle, 2008), such as microbreaks to muscle fibres. In response, the body regenerates stronger (Beachle and Earle, 2008) and adapts to this stress. In our example the muscle fibres repair even stronger than before so that the next time the body is put under this stress it does not become damaged. In order for this regeneration to occur the body requires adequate time to repair (Beachle and Earle, 2008), this time varying according to the degree of stress placed on it. Powerful and explosive actions require twenty four hours for recovery (Beachle and Earle, 2008), as these actions fatigue the neuromuscular system, whereas resistance based weight exercises require up to seventy two hours for recovery (Beachle and Earle, 2008), as these exercises fatigue the musculoskeletal system. Soccer involves a mix of explosive actions and intense loading; thus recovering from a match or conditioning soccer session can take forty eight hours (Buchheit et al., 2015).

Using this adaptation philosophy, training can be periodised to overload the body slowly so that it is stressed, recovers and regenerates even stronger. Repeating this cycle in an appropriate manner will enhance the physical qualities of young soccer players and is the basis of periodisation within elite youth soccer. It is important that the stress is at an appropriate overload to ensure that it does not cause injury and the recovery time needs to be adequate to allow full regeneration, otherwise the risks of fatigue and injury are increased (Beachle and Earle, 2008). When developing functional capacity, the body is overloaded with gym exercises, field exercises and soccer conditioning drills. To reach this stage where functional capacity can be developed it is first important to develop the movement base and then progress the exercises this base allows the player to perform. Doing so will allow the player to exit their PHV capable of immediately developing functional capacity.

Planning and periodisation will be progressed throughout the phases. The U8-U10 planning and periodisation ensures that the exercises progress in the correct way, building from the basic fundamental movement skills, such as a squat. Within this age group we are teaching technique, and the focus of periodising is to ensure that all the fundamental movements are covered within the phase. Periodising the themes within your weeks and months will therefore be adequate (examples are given in the phase chapter). Developing the fundamental movement skills and functional competency within these phases ensures an excellent movement base is achieved and can now be progressed.

The U11–U13 phase introduces the players to more structured training, and as a result the sets and reps of exercises need to be planned and periodised (examples of this process are included within the phase chapter). The weeks and months can also be periodised to ensure that the fundamentals learnt during the U8–U10 phase are progressively developed, with the gym exercises becoming more advanced and the fundamental movement skills becoming more soccer specific. This phase of periodisation develops the players' understanding and ability to perform structured training, allowing them to easily adapt to the next phase of developing functional capacity.

The planning and periodisation within the U14–U16 phase ensures that the players are developing their functional capacity; ability to perform fundamental movements with greater speed, strength and power. The greater exposure a coach gets with these age groups allows them to introduce periodisation of the days, weeks and training cycles. The focus is now to overload the physical capabilities of the players using the excellent movement base developed within the earlier phases. The days will become periodised to ensure that optimal adaptation occurs through more specific training. Time is optimised by including upper body and lower body gym sessions within the week, whilst soccer conditioning through small sided games is introduced. Examples of this periodisation will be found in the U14–U16 chapter. The intensity of matches now means that lower body gym and soccer conditioning within training have to be appropriately placed within the week to prevent overstressing the body during the forty eight hours it is still recovering. The high intensity of conditioning training sessions also means that it is important to ensure that the players are not fatigued going into matches. As discussed, the physical development of young soccer players not only requires adequate overload but also adequate time for the body to recover and regenerate. The training cycles are periodised to ensure that the field based strength and conditioning sessions compliment the training performed within the gym, thus optimising physical development. For example, speed work in the gym will be performed whilst field based sessions develop speed. Overload within sessions now takes place through an increase in sets, reps and, where applicable, resistance, rather than a progression in exercise as performed within the earlier phases. The most important factor to consider during this phase is PHV and the associated temporary losses in coordination, mobility and body awareness. As a result, the planning and periodisation of players needs to be individualised and adapted depending on a player's maturation. The planning of a session may now require three players to perform different exercises within the same session theme.

The book's philosophy on planning and periodisation incorporates the findings of scientific research, and the phases within the book will guide coaches through the correct planning and periodisation required to develop the physical characteristics of elite young soccer players.

RECOVERY STRATEGIES

Both soccer training and games put a high physical strain on the body (Wallace et al., 2014); with the intense schedule usually undertaken it is essential to implement recovery strategies. This will help the players to recover quicker from the last session, and hence perform better in the next. It will also help to reduce the risk of injury and illness. You want your players to be as fresh as possible for every single session because that gives them the best chance to train harder and get better. By commencing the use of these strategies from a young age you will embed these good habits and they will become the norm.

Recovery starts the moment the session ends or the final whistle blows. Performing a cool down for fifteen to thirty minutes afterwards will help to begin the recovery process (Tessitore et al., 2007).

Cool Down:
- Light Jog – 5 minutes
- Dynamic Mobility – 10 minutes (x10 each side)
  - Calves
  - Hamstrings
  - Quadriceps
  - Hip Flexors
  - Groins
  - Glutes
- Static Mobility – 10 minutes (each stretch 1 minute each side)
  - Calves
  - Hamstring
  - Quadriceps
  - Hip Flexors
  - Groins
  - Glutes

These mobility exercises should also be performed by the players on days they are not training in order to prevent stiffness and tightness in the muscles (this links to the corrective exercises within the Functional Competence Chapter).

Nutrition not only affects recovery and subsequent performance but also growth, so the implementation of a correct nutrition plan is essential for an adolescent soccer player (Loucks, 2004). This nutrition plan should not be only for game or training days, it should be a lifelong regime and this will come with time as they gain a better understanding of what they should be eating. Here the education of parents is also important because they will be the ones feeding the child. By starting at a young age you will be setting good habits for them to continue when they are older. Providing parents and players with pre- and post-game nutrition intake sheets, as well as guidelines to good and bad foods for everyday life, are excellent tools to help guide them to what they should be eating. Examples of what can be included in pre- and post-game nutrition intake sheets are shown below.

Pre-game intake

o   2-3 hours pre-game – Low Glycemic Index (GI) carbohydrate meal (pasta, toast, fruit juice) with a medium portion of protein (eggs, meat, fish, beans/pulses, spreads) and water (1 pint).
o   30 minutes pre-game – High GI carbohydrate drink or food (energy drink, jaffa cakes, jelly babies) and water.

Post-game intake

o   Immediately post-game – High GI carbohydrate drink or food (energy drink, jaffa cakes, jelly babies) and water (1 pint).
o   2 hours post game – Meal containing complex carbohydrates (brown pasta, brown rice, jacket potato) protein (meat, fish, eggs, high protein beans/pulses) vegetables (try to create a colourful selection) and water.
o   Before bed – slow release protein (milk, yoghurt).

AGES 8-10

Would you build a house without foundations? So why would you try to produce an elite soccer player without having those building blocks in place? The work done between the ages of 8–10 is pivotal within the development process. Neglecting to look at physical development during this phase will not prepare the players for future years, thus placing them at a disadvantage in reaching their potential.

This phase of development comes before the occurrence of any major growth spurt, although this does not mean they are not growing and some players may begin to suffer from growth related conditions such as Sever's disease. Close attention must be taken to movement patterns during this phase in order to identify these early, as many young players will continue to train and play without mentioning an injury which may cause lasting damage, affecting their long term development.

Players from this age band are generally the most difficult to coach, because at such a young age they have low attention spans, are easily excitable and have an abundance of energy. However, they are the most rewarding, because massive changes can be seen very quickly as the players are 'blank canvases'. You need the players to be enthusiastic about the sessions themselves; if they do not enjoy them it is highly likely they will not take part properly, and may maintain this negative view of physical training throughout their career. It is essential, therefore, to create a fun game orientated way of learning, which keeps them on the move and captivated with a variety of learning objectives from the session. Players at this age will respond best to a visual coaching aid, so good demonstrations are pivotal, because they see something and copy it. It is also important to allow players to use 'trial and error' at times, because if they try something and fail owing to poor technique they are less likely to repeat it. This will help reinforce good technique and the desire to learn it.

FUNCTIONAL COMPETENCE

At the age of 8–10 players should have a good level of mobility, because there is relatively little in the way of muscle size and definition yet. Lack of mobility at this age range is usually a neuromuscular issue whereby their bodies are not used to going through that range of motion. Static stretching is the obvious protocol with which many link the development of mobility; however, in this age band simply going through the full range of motion around joints is an effective tool in developing neuromuscular mobility; it will also aid in maintaining mobility as the players grow.

Mobility is primarily affected by growth and maturation, so it is important that from a young age a maintenance programme is put in place, in order that the players do not lose mobility as they get older. This links into weight training preparation, whereby we can begin to teach the players the technical foundations of key movements, whilst also helping to maintain and improve necessary functional competences such as mobility and stability. The key movements we would want our 8–10 year olds to begin to understand and have the ability to master are listed below.

Key Exercises:

o Squat
o Lunge
o Clean

At this stage we want to develop the understanding of a triple extension (jump-like movement) with the feet jumping out slightly to land in a front squat position.

o Snatch

At this stage we want to develop the understanding of a triple extension (jump-like movement) with the feet jumping out slightly and arms extended overhead.

o Jerk

At this stage we want to develop the understanding of a knee dip and drive movement to land into the split squat (e.g. lunge position) with the arms extended directly above the head.

Fun games which involve these specific movements are effective in getting the players to learn and understand the movements. By making the games competitive it can also encourage the players to practise at home because they will want to beat their team mates the next time.

Drill 1 – Fun Open Drill – 'Squatting Limbo'

Drill Aim – Squatting Technique

Have the players spread out around a small area, with enough space between each so they are able to squat down. Once each one has a place, using a rope (you holding one end and an assistant the other) and starting from a high level which is easy to squat under, walk from one end to the other making the players squat under the rope. Emphasise good technique (straight back, feet flat, flexion of hips and knees): they are out if the technique is poor rather than simply being unable to get under the rope. Each time you reach the other end the height of the rope should be lowered, making it more and more difficult. The last player left is the winner.

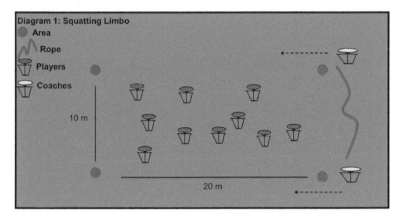

Sets: 2–4   *Reps:* N/A
Recovery: 1–2 minutes

Progression

The squats can be progressed to all variations (shown in the next chapter), away from the game environment. The sets and reps should be low because the aim is to work on technique rather than any sort of physical adaptation.

Regression

If a player is unable to squat this may be caused by a functional issue, such as tight hips, tight calves, etc. However, at this young age the usual reason is that they have not learnt the movement yet. Taking them out of the game environment and giving them coaching queues specific to them should be sufficient. (e.g. 'keep heels on the floor', 'chest and head up', 'push your knees out')

Common technical errors to look for:

o   Heels raised
o   Back arches
o   Knees move in

Drill Aim – Lunging Technique

Get the players to separate into teams, and have them work from one cone to another (ten metres) as a team performing lunges in unison. One team member should give the shouts (forward, down, up, step) so the movement is broken down. Otherwise you will find a lot of players' knees shifting forward and the rear of their front feet coming up. Emphasise technique: front foot flat, bend back leg to go straight down, chest tall, flat back. Give out points to teams who perform technique correctly. Winning team has the most points.

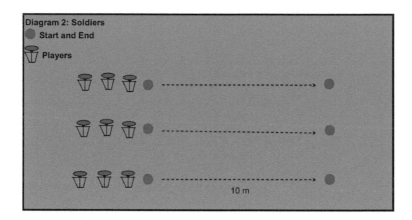

Sets: 2-4   *Reps:* 10 m
Recovery: 1-2 minutes between sets

Progression

The march can incorporate lunge variations such as backwards and sideways, which involve similar technical points, only the direction of the first step varies.

Regression

If a player is unable to perform a lunge it is again most probably the result of an unlearned movement. Taking them out of the game environment and giving them coaching queues specific to them should be sufficient. (e.g. 'straight down', 'chest and head up', 'bend back leg')

Common technical errors to look for:
o   Front heel raised
o   Front knee comes forward
o   Upper body falls forward

Drill Aim – Olympic Lifting Technique

Have the players partner up, the first game is:

Cowboys

This is designed to develop the clean technique, and you will tell the players to be cowboys, in a shooting showdown with their partner. They must start back to back, hands by their side as if clutching their gun. On GO they slowly walk away from each other; on TURN they turn and face still keeping hands by their side, but now get them to go into a ready position (say, 'Standing upright isn't a very reactive positon so you'll get shot'). Have the players get into a slight knee bend and hip hinge. Then, on the shout FIRE, the quickest cowboy to get his guns up to his shoulders with a little jump up and out of his feet, landing in a low body position, wins.

The second game is:

Starfish

This helps to develop the snatch technique. This time the players start face to face, with a two metre gap between them. The game is a best of three knock out competition. Both players must start in the ready position as above, this time with hands out straight by the sides of the body. On GO they must get into a starfish position, hands out stretched over head and in a squat position. First player into the position gets the point. Winners can then pair up and go against each other.

The final game is:

Waiters

This develops the jerk technique. The players can now move around a marked out area pretending to be waiters holding imaginary plates at their shoulders. Then, all of a sudden, there is an EARTHQUAKE!!! The ground starts to split underneath them. So the players must jump into a split leg position, one foot in front flat and other behind on the balls of the feet, with arms outstretched above the head, keeping the plates from falling.

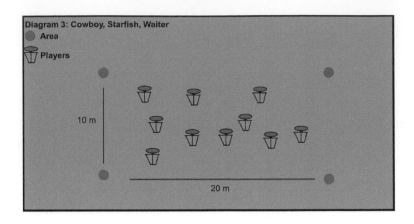

Diagram 3: Cowboy, Starfish, Waiter
● Area
♔ Players

10 m

20 m

Sets: 3–6 *Reps:* 3–6
Recovery: 1–2 minutes

Progression
The lifts can be progressed with the use of dowels to perform the movements, still not breaking down the lift too much and just allowing the players to experiment and attempt to get into the right positions.

Regression
If a player is unable to perform the movements, go back to simple squatting and lunging games to build a greater base of functional competence before advancing to these more difficult movements.

FUNDAMENTAL MOVEMENT SKILLS

By the ages of 8–10 players would have performed the majority of the fundamental movements in everyday life, usually with friends in unstructured play. Therefore, when coaching fundamental movement skills at this age we are not necessarily teaching something new but refining what a player can already do and making it more effective and efficient. No one would have told them how to run or how to jump before, and if you observe two players they may move very differently. There is no single ideal way to move because there are always anomalies. However, there are basic technical points which if learned by the player can enhance the effectiveness and efficiency of their movements. We are not teaching them how to run because they can already run; we are refining their running technique through basic technical adjustments.

During this first phase of teaching acceleration, deceleration and agility the exercises are performed in a fun environment and develop these basic athletic actions. The basics to any movement are important, so to start you need to break down the basic technical points to make simple drills.

ACCELERATION

Drill 1 – Closed Drill

Drill Aim – Foot Patterns

A simple drill that can teach the small to big foot patterns is to get a pile of cones, and ask the players to put them out from a start cone on how their footsteps should be when they accelerate out. This is a trial and error way of learning. Let them put the cones out and try and run through them a few times. If there is more than one group, they can switch lines and run through each-other's and give good and bad points so that when they go back to their line they can make adjustments. As the coach you should help with some pointers at this stage, before allowing them to run through the cones a few times to get used to this small to big step pattern.

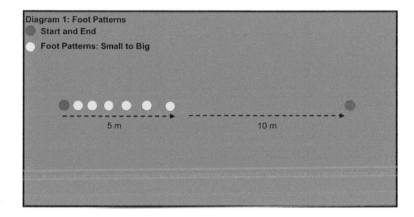

Sets: 3-6   *Reps:* 1-3

Recovery: 2-3 minutes between sets, 10-20 seconds between reps.

Progression

Remove the cones and get the players to accelerate out, using that same foot pattern of small to big. You can get the players in pairs, so that the partner can watch the start and give their partner thumbs up if they used correct technique or thumbs down if they did not.

Regression

The coach sets the cones to the desirable distance for small to big foot patterns, and initially gets the players to go through at 60-70% speed. Slowing down the movement will emphasise good technique.

Common technical errors to look for:

o   Over reaching with first few steps

o   Not elongating steps and just moving feet really fast as they continue to accelerate out

Drill Aim – Body Height

Start the players lying flat on the floor on their stomachs. On a shout they must get up as quickly as possible. The majority will just get up and stand upright. This is where as a coach you need to emphasise the importance of getting up into a sprinting stance. Repeat the exercise; hopefully, they will now rise first into a press up position with legs split (one knee bent, one extended) and then into a sprinting position. If they understand the way of getting up then allow for three steps out after rising on the next go, so as to begin accelerating.

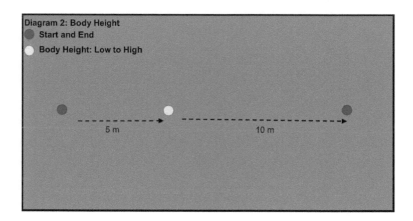

Sets: 3-6   *Reps:* 1-3

Recovery: 2-3 minutes between sets, 10-20 seconds between reps.

Progression 1

Once the technique of rising is grasped get the players to start on their stomachs, rise, and accelerate out ten metres.

Progression 2

Now you can make the drill more open by getting the players to pair up and play a game of cat and mouse. They both lie on their stomachs with the second player a metre behind the first player. At the shout of GO the player behind must catch the player in front over ten metres. They can then walk back and switch roles.

Regression

If the player is struggling to get in the correct initial position, have them stay in the press-up position on the floor, alternating legs in a piston like action to mimic the driving phase of the first steps.

Common technical errors to look for:
o   Stands upright before sprinting out
o   Will not have legs split when getting up

Drill 3 – Fun Open Drill – 'Crocodiles'

Drill Aim – Acceleration (and Agility)

This drill will work on both agility and acceleration skills for the players. Have a rectangular area with a smaller square in the middle. Pick two players to be the crocodiles and have them lie on their stomachs in the smaller square. The rest of the squad should be on one end of the rectangle; their aim is to run as fast as they can to the other end without being eaten by the crocodiles. Once they reach the other end the crocodiles must re-enter their square and re-start on their stomachs. As soon as the first player runs the crocodiles can get up and try to catch them, this will practice the body height low to high technique. The players that are caught become crocodiles; last player standing is the winner. The game can then be re-started with the winner and one other player beginning as crocodiles.

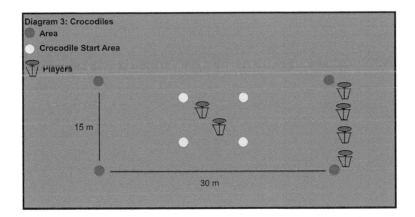

Games: 2-4   *Reps*: N/A
Recovery: 2-3 minutes between games.

DECELERATION

Drill 1 – Closed Drill

Drill Aim – Foot Patterns

Similar to the acceleration drill, give the players a pile of six cones and get them to place the cones in what they believe should be their foot patterns when coming to a stop on an end cone. Follow the same routine as above. The starting point should be about fifteen metres from the end point. When stopping at the end cone, you want the players to be in a quarter squat position (so feet slightly wider than shoulder width, knees in line with toes, weight in mid-foot, straight back, head up).

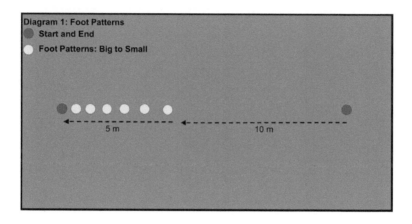

Sets: 3-6   *Reps:* 1-3

Recovery: 2-3 minutes between sets, 10-20 seconds between reps.

Progression

The drill can become more open by now giving a verbal or visual stimulus in order to stop. Get the players to sprint out and on a shout of STOP they must decelerate and come to a stop as quickly as possible. The stimulus can vary to hand signals, body movements, etc.

Regression

The coach sets the cones up to the desirable distance for big to small foot patterns, and initially gets the players to go through at 60-70% speed. Slowing down the movement will emphasise good technique.

Common technical errors to look for:

o   Not a stable end positon
o   No real shortening of footsteps in anticipation of stop

Drill Aim – Body Height

Get the players moving around a large area. Then, on a shout, the players must get down to the floor as quickly as possible and lie on their stomachs. On a second shout they must accelerate back up and continue moving around the area.

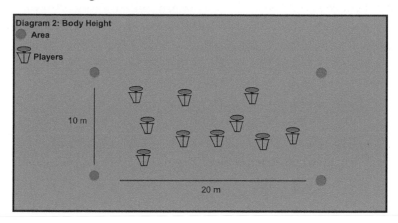

Sets: 3-5   *Reps:* 1-3

Recovery: 2-3 minutes between sets, 10-20 seconds between reps.

Progression

Have the players move around the area, but this time, on a shout, the player must stop as quickly as possible in a low body position. Emphasise the quarter squat position when at a stop. This can then rotate to a half turn stop, because the player does not want to be square when decelerating to an opponent. The feet need to be slightly wider than shoulder width, to allow for a powerful stance to accelerate out again.

Regression

Rather than having them moving around, get the players to be on the spot and drop down into that quarter squat position on a shout. Emphasise knees in line with toes, feet slightly wider than shoulder width, head up, straight back, mid foot (so ready to accelerate).

Common technical errors to look for:

o   Feet too close

o   Standing upright

o   Not stable

Once the player has grasped the basic technical points on how to start (accelerate) and stop (decelerate) the transition between the two phases can be worked on. This transition is known as a player's Agility.

AGILITY

Drill 1 – Fun Open Drill – 'Bulldog'

Drill Aim – Agility

Pick two players to be bulldogs, with the rest of the squad at one end of the area. On the bulldogs' shout, the other players must run to the other end without being tagged. If tagged, they become bulldogs. Last player left is the winner.

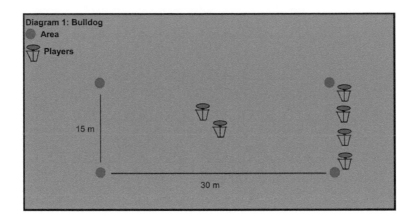

Games: 2-4   *Reps*: N/A

Recovery: 2-3 minutes between games.

Drill 2 – Fun Open Drill – 'Tag Football'

Drill Aim – Agility (Hand-eye Co-ordination, Reaction Skills)

Split the players into small sided teams, and number the teams. Every time you shout two numbers, the teams must run to the end zone pointed out when the number is called. First team there gets possession and can begin throwing the ball to each other. Once possession is gained the players must try to get into the end zone with the ball. If not tagged the ball can be passed forwards or backwards; once tagged the ball can only go backwards. Possession switches only when ball is intercepted or goes out of play. Put a time constraint on the game, so the intensity remains high. First team to get into opposition end zone wins, and then two new numbers are called.

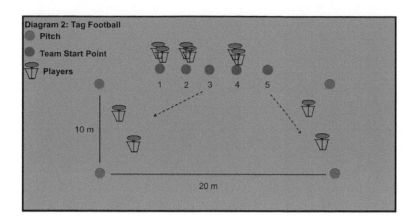

Games: 2-4 per team   *Reps:* 1-2 minutes

Recovery: 2-3 minutes between games.

Drill 3 – 'The Square'

Drill Aim – Agility

Set up a small square per two players, each cone having a number (1,2,3,4). One player will be working and the other resting. When in the square the player should be in a quarter squat position, as mentioned earlier, because it gives them a powerful stance. The player's body shape should be facing forwards throughout the drill. The player starts in the middle; on the shout of a number the player must go to the cone, then return to the middle.

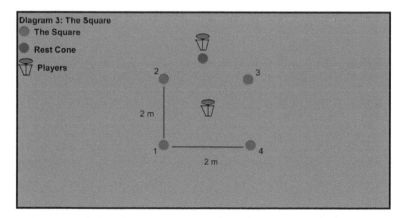

Sets: 3-6   *Reps:* 1 (30 seconds)

Recovery: 1-2 minutes between sets

Progression

Have two squares which are facing each other. Player two must mirror player one's movements.

They then alternate. This is also good to emphasise the forward facing chest and eyes, because if the player turns their back they will not be able to mirror their partner.

Regression

If the player is struggling to maintain the forward facing, low body shape when moving to the cones, pull them out of the drill and get them to perform the same movements at 60% speed. This will help them to figure out how to move in a less pressurised environment.

PLYOMETRIC

Drill 1 – Fun Open Drill – 'Surfing'

Drill Aim – Jumping and Landing

Set up a large area which the players can move around pretending to be surfing (arms moving while jogging around). On a shout of WAVE they must freeze and get into a jump ready position (feet shoulder width apart). Then, with a long rope (you holding one end and a colleague the other), walk from one end of the area to the other, making the players jump over the rope. If a player does not make it over, they are out. They should not take a run up for the jump; they should be still and jump over the rope as it passes beneath them. They are also out if they land with poor technique (use technical points from the Fundamental Movement Skills Chapter). Once the rope reaches the other end shout SURF, so the players can begin to move around the area again. Increase the rope height each time, to increase the difficulty. Players drop out if they cannot make the jump or land with poor technique. Last player left is the winner.

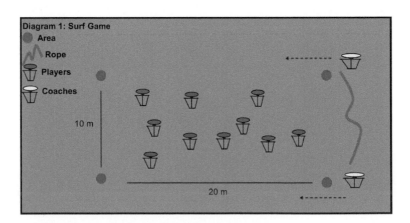

Sets: 1 – 3   *Reps:* N/A
Recovery: 1-2 minutes

Progression

Rather than double leg, the drill can become single leg. Have the players moving around the area. On the shout of WAVE they must balance on one leg. When the rope passes beneath them they must hop and land onto the same leg. They can only go back onto two legs when SURF is shouted. Again, they drop out if they land with poor technique (same technical points when landing on one leg as with double leg) or do not make the jump. The height of the rope must be a lot lower during this game because it is a single leg exercise, so make sure it is an attainable height for your players.

Regression

If the player is struggling with the fundamentals of landing have them just standing on the spot, and dropping down to a quarter squat position, weight in the mid foot, back straight, feet shoulder width, as quickly as possible. This will get them used to getting into the appropriate landing position.

Common technical errors to look for:

o   Landing on heels or toes
o   Not sinking into landing (no knee or hip bend)
o   Top half of body falls forward

Drill 2 – Fun Open Drill – 'Leap Frogs'

Drill Aim – Jumping and Landing

Set up an area with circular discs (cones or hula-hoops) spread out within, with varying distances and angles between them. The players must then jump from one circle to another to reach the other side; if they fail to reach a circle they are out because they have fallen in 'the pond'. There should be multiple routes to get over the pond, and the players should vary the route each time they try. More than one player can go at a time, in order to force players to go certain ways. Try not to over coach the drill; let the players learn for themselves – just slip in coaching points such as, 'I don't want to hear your landings'.

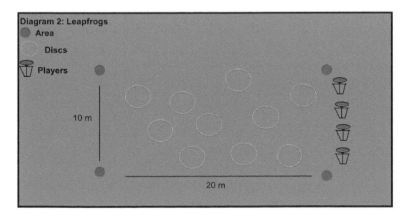

Sets: 3-5   *Reps:* N/A
Recovery: 1-2 minutes between sets

Progression

Rather than double leg, the drill can become single leg. Have the players hop from circle to circle. The distances will have to be made smaller between circles prior to starting.

Regression

If a player struggles with the fundamentals of jumping, the movement can be broken down to sections. First get the player to stretch up as far as they can, arms above their head and on their tip-toes (feet shoulder width). Using the phrase 'like a pencil' can help them to visualise the correct stance. On a shout of GO get the players to drop down into a quarter squat position, weight now in the mid foot and arms down by their sides 'like a slalom skier'. On the shout of GO again they return to the first position. By speeding up the shout they will then mimic the jumping motion. Finally, allow them to combine the two movements and perform a jump.

Common technical errors to look for:

o   Not using arms to help jump
o   No countermovement
o   Feet too close or too far apart

Drill 3 – Closed Drill – 'Hurdle Jumps'

Drill Aim – Jump Height and Landing
Set out four hurdles, the height dependent on the ability and height of players. You want the players to jump high over the hurdles in a quick counter movement jump. The landings must be soft and stable, with a few seconds hold before they jump the next one.

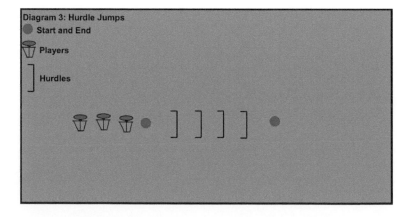

50

Sets: 3-5   *Reps:* 4
Recovery: 2-3 minutes between sets

Progression
Increase the height of the hurdles.

Regression
Decrease the height of the hurdles or even remove them, in order to re-emphasise technique.

Common technical errors to look for:
o   Pushing legs out wide to pass hurdle rather than going over
o   Not pulling legs up when jumping
o   No arm and leg co-ordination to help momentum

Drill 4 – Closed Drill – 'Ladder Hops'

Drill Aim – Single Leg Balance, Jumping and Landing
Put out a ladder and get the players to hop and hold through it. The technical points are similar; however, now it is just jumping and landing on one leg. Variations can be used through the ladder so the jumps are forwards, backwards, sideways and diagonal. You do not want to do too many repetitions: four-six are sufficient because technique is lost once the leg is fatigued.

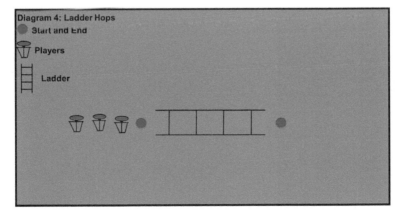

Sets: 3-5   *Reps:* 4-6
Recovery: 2-3 minutes between sets

Progression
Introducing mini-hurdles rather than a ladder to get greater height on the hops.

Regression

Having the player practise single leg balance exercises in order to increase stability in the leg, which will make it more solid for jumping and landing.

Common technical errors to look for:

o   Foot and knee instability so body moves
o   Failure to bend at both hip and knee to cushion landing and be stable
o   Leaving arms down by side instead of using them as a tool to help jumping and stability

PLANNING AND PERIODISATION

Depending upon the amount of time you have for a session, the choice of drills and aims will be affected. At this age you want to begin exposing the players to all the exercises and skills through fun environments, so putting together a scheme of work as shown below is a simple means of monitoring whether each player has experienced, understood and can execute each functional and fundamental requirement prior to entering the next phase of their development.

Scheme of work:

- Mobility
    - Gym exercises
        - Squat
        - Lunge
        - Olympic lifts

- Stability
    - Single leg balance
    - Landing
        - Double leg
        - Single leg
    - Core

- Co-ordination
    - Hand – eye
    - Arms – legs

- Reaction Skills
    - Single limbs
    - Whole body

- ➤ Ability to Jump
  - o Double leg
  - o Single leg

- ➤ Ability to Accelerate
  - o Foot patterns
  - o Body height

- ➤ Ability to Decelerate
  - o Foot patterns
  - o Body height

- ➤ Changing Direction
  - o Linear
  - o Multi-directional

This will place them in an excellent place to progress further in the next phase.

There is no single right way to structure sessions for this age range. However, a beneficial structure, in both time efficiency and learning effectiveness, is the use of circuits. Circuits can be a useful tool in creating a fun way of learning and allowing the players to experience a variety of exercises from the above scheme of work within one session.

Circuit Drill – Fun Open Drills

Drill Aim – Functional Competence and Fundamental Movement Skills
  Station 1: Double leg jumping and landing – *leapfrogs*
  Station 2: Single leg balance – *whilst throwing and catching ball with partner*
  Station 3: Core – *battle planks*
  Station 4: Mobility – *squatting limbo*
  Station 5: Co-ordination/Reaction skills – *throw and catch reaction, ball off wall*
  Station 6: Speed – *cat and mouse*

The six stations can vary and the exercises can be chosen from the examples above, together with other exercises appropriate to those categories.

Sets: 1-2   *Reps:* 1-2 minutes
Recovery: walk to next station

Below is an example of a possible training week for an 8–10 year old player, with a download week placed every fourth week, where session intensity is reduced, in order to allow for physical regeneration.

Example Week:

Match Day	No Training	Training Day 1	No Training	Training Day 2	No Training	Training Day 3
No S&C		Competition Circuit		Fun Field based Games		Warm Up – Mobility, Stability

Preferably, the physical development work should take place at the start of a session for twenty to thirty minutes when the players are fresh. Understandably, amateur clubs may only get contact with their players for one session a week, the session being the day prior to a game, and that is where the games and competition circuit can be combined and shortened to fit at the start of that session.

SOCCER SPECIFIC PREPARATION

The building of good habits starts now so the implementation of cool downs after sessions, even if only for ten minutes, begins to get the players used to what they should be doing. We must emphasise again that providing the players/parents with guidelines on nutrition is important in establishing good habits straight away, because it will get harder to do so as players get older.

AGES 11–13

We have now built the foundations of our soccer players and the ages 11–13 years offer an opportunity to develop the fundamental movement skills learnt within this initial phase and make them more specific to soccer. The nature of sessions can now become more structured as the players' concentration skills progress. This phase allows us to teach the players how to train.

As previously mentioned, the average age for PHV, adolescent growth spurt, in young males is 13.8 years of age, which falls outside the age range for this phase of development. By simply looking at the players within your own squads it will clearly be seen that they still vary in their rate of growth. It is therefore important not to use a 'one size fits all' approach to the physical development of young soccer players.

The majority of 11–13 year old boys will be at the pre- PHV phase of development. It is important to begin to develop the good habits of undertaking functional competency work away from the training ground during this period, as this will not only establish a good mind set during later years but also physically place them in good condition when entering their PHV.

A child who is advanced in maturity will begin to experience the effects of this rapid growth earlier than 13 years of age. A player advanced in maturity, and with excellent technique at the weightlifting exercises and fundamental movement drills within this phase, should follow the 14-16 training guidelines, as they are biologically ready for the next stage of their physical development.

FUNCTIONAL COMPETENCE

During the earlier ages of 8–10 years, the basics of functional competency are developed, so during the ages of 11–13 the players will now build upon this base. Developing this functional competency is important in these age groups as it prepares them before they approach their PHV.

This progress and maintenance in functional competency can be achieved through regularly completing exercises that target the common areas of weakness among young soccer players.

In terms of exercise prescription, the exercises are more structured in nature. The importance within this phase is to ensure the players perform the exercises with the correct technique and begin to understand how to activate certain muscle groups when performing an action.

Mobility and Stability Exercise Index:

	Exercise	Sets	Reps
Core	Deadbug	2	6–10
	Plank	2	30–60 seconds
	Side Plank	2 each side	20–40 seconds
	Quadruped Exercise	2 each side	6–10
Glutes	Clam	2	6–10
	Glute Bridge	2	6–10
	Single Leg Glute Bridge	2 each leg	6–10
	Band Walk Progression	2 each side	10 metres
Proprioception	Single Leg Balance	2 each side	30–60 seconds
Calf Mobility	Foam Roll	Each side	60–120 seconds
	Stretch 1	Each side	60–120 seconds
	Stretch 2	Each side	60–120 seconds
Hip Flexors	Foam Roll	Each side	60–120 seconds
	Stretch	Each side	60–120 seconds
	Hurdle Walk	2 each side	8–12

WEIGHT TRAINING

During the ages of 8–10 the players would have developed a strong fundamental movement base, which now allows for more specific exercise preparation. Derivatives of the exercises can be completed using a dowel and then progressed to a training bar. Throughout this phase of development, the emphasis is on technique and the coach should never compromise a child's technique to compensate for load.

Players will have developed a basic understanding of the squat, lunge, snatch and clean and jerk movement patterns. This will have been done in a fun environment and will now be developed into more structured exercise. Exercises within this phase's exercise index will either be progressed by being performed as a different variation or by being performed with a dowel or training bar.

Key Exercises:

- ➢ Squat
  - o Back Squat
  - o Front Squat
  - o Overhead Squat

The aim within this phase is to develop the basic squat pattern the players learnt within the fun games into the more recognized exercises of back squat, front squat and overhead squat.

- ➢ Lunge
  - o Forward Lunge
  - o Reverse Lunge
  - o Side Lunge

The players will have an understanding of the lunge pattern. Players who perform these exercises with excellent technique can be challenged with the addition of a dowel or training bar held on the shoulders, or overhead, throughout the exercise.

- ➢ Deadlift
  - o Training Bar Deadlift
  - o Romanian Deadlift
  - o Single Leg Romanian Deadlift

The deadlift represents a new exercise that will be taught within this phase. Utilizing the squatting pattern, developed within the previous phase, players will learn how to perform the ordinary deadlift as well as the Romanian and single leg Romanian derivatives. Teaching the players how to perform the deadlift will ensure they know how to correctly lift weight from the ground and return it, ensuring good habits are developed, important for the later phases when the weight on the bar will be increased.

- ➢ Snatch
  - o Hang Snatch

The aim within this phase is to progress the triple extension taught within the previous phase, so that the players are able to perform a hang snatch with a dowel or training bar.

- Clean
  - o Hang Clean

The aim within this phase is to progress the triple extension taught within the previous phase, so that the players are able to perform a hang clean with a dowel or training bar.

- Jerk
  - o Jerk from Shoulders

The aim within this phase is to progress the knee dip and triple extension taught within the previous phase, so that the players are able to perform a jerk from shoulders with a dowel or training bar.

Once the player can perform the above exercises with the correct technique, using a dowel, for every rep, they are ready to progress to the training bar. Throughout this phase the coach should be technique led when teaching these complicated multi-joint exercises, not moving to the next progression until the current one can be performed correctly, repetition after repetition.

Example Sessions:

Session 1
Aim – Develop Deadlift and Back Squat Technique

Exercise	Sets	Reps	Rest between sets
Back Squat Technique	3	5	1 mlnute
Deadlift Technique	3	5	1 minute
Walking Lunge	3	6 each leg	1 minute

Session 2
Aim – Develop Clean and Jerk Technique

Exercise	Sets	Reps	Rest between sets
Front Squat Technique	3	5	1 minute
Hang Clean Technique	3	3	1 minute
Jerk Technique	3	2 each leg	1 minute

Session 3
Aim – Develop Snatch Technique

Exercise	Sets	Reps	Rest between sets
Overhead Squat Technique	3	5	1 minute
Hang Snatch Technique	3	3	1 minute
Romanian Deadlift	3	5	1 minute

FUNDAMENTAL MOVEMENT SKILLS

Like functional competency the basic fundamental movement skills have been developed at the ages of 8–10. The next step in the development of the players' movement skills is to make the training more specific to soccer. The training performed during that first phase is undertaken in a fun environment in order to match the attention capacity of the child, but as players become older they are able to take part in training that is more structured. It is, however, crucial to make sure that an enjoyable environment for the players is still maintained, as you want to ensure they do not lose enthusiasm within the sessions at this early stage of their physical development.

During the early phases of teaching acceleration, deceleration and agility, the exercises were performed in an athletic action. Now we will begin to perform them in a soccer specific action.

ACCELERATION

Drill 1 – Closed Drill

Drill Aim – Accelerate from Soccer Specific Jockey Position
Utilising the keys to acceleration taught during the early acceleration drills, get the players to stand in the position they would if they were going to close an individual down, the jockey position (as shown in the Fundamental Movement Skills Chapter). Ask them which foot they would make the first step with? Let them try accelerating off both the front and back foot. Then guide them towards the answer, using the information they learnt from earlier acceleration drills: 'a small first step from the back foot'.

Ask them why it is a small step and from the back foot? Or again get them to try it out. A learning environment in which they are guided towards the answer is a much better way of teaching players of this age than telling them how things should be done. It will also promote a positive learning environment in which to acquire the strength and conditioning that will benefit them throughout their physical development.

Once the players have reached the conclusion that a small first step should be taken from the back foot, they can perform accelerations from this position.

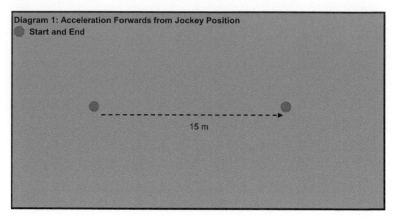

Diagram 1: Acceleration Forwards from Jockey Position

Sets: 3-6   *Reps:* 1–3

Recovery: 2-3 minutes between sets, 10-20 seconds between reps.

Progression

To progress the exercise, it can become open in nature, the players reacting to a team mate, whom they have to chase, or from a shout. This will make the action more specific to soccer as, ultimately, within a match you make accelerations in reaction to other stimuli.

Regression

If a player is struggling to achieve the desired step pattern from the jockey position, you can add the cones from drill one of the U8 – U10 phase. Once they are able to sprint through the cones with the correct step pattern they can then begin to perform it with fewer cones, slowly progressing to no cones.

Common technical errors to look for:

o   Player does not lead with back leg
o   Player is positioned too side on or not side on enough
o   Player forgets foot pattern and body height

Drill 2 – Closed Drill

Drill Aim – Accelerate from Soccer Specific Jockey Position in the Direction they are not Facing
Soccer involves many changes of direction and, as a result, it is important players are able to accelerate forwards from the jockey position, as in Drill 1, but also accelerate back in the direction they are not facing.

As in Drill 1, guide the players to the correct movement pattern, with the front foot now coming around the body, turning the way they are facing, and performing a small first step (as shown in Fundamental Movement Skills Chapter). But again get them to try the different movements so they know how the correct movement pattern feels.

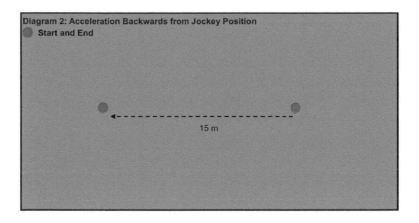

Diagram 2: Acceleration Backwards from Jockey Position
Start and End
15 m

Sets: 3-6   *Reps:* 1–3

Recovery: 2-3 minutes between sets, 10-20 seconds between reps.

Progression

To progress this drill players pair up facing each other, two metres apart, in the jockey position. Reacting to a call, their partner or another stimulus, one player accelerates forward, using the skills learnt from Drill 1 and the other player turns and accelerates from the jockey position, using the skills learnt in Drill 2. The player who has turned, has to sprint over a line ten metres away before being caught by their partner. Players can have a bib hanging from their shorts, which must be taken, or simply be tagged.

Regression

To regress this drill, cones can be laid out in the correct step pattern to help the player accelerate away in the correct manner. Once they are able to perform the drill correctly with cones, the number of cones can begin to be reduced until the player is performing the drill correctly without any cones.

Common technical errors to look for:

o   Player turns the wrong way
o   Player is positioned too side on or not side on enough
o   Player forgets foot patterns and body height

Drill Aim – Acceleration from Movement Box

This drill will aim to utilise the skills learnt in Drill 1 and 2 but progress it to become even more soccer specific. Thus far the players have been performing the exercises from a stationary position, but within soccer a player will rarely find themselves standing still.

This drill finds the players in a small box, with four different coloured cones at each corner. To begin with the player has to jockey to the cone that is called and then jockey back to the middle point of the square, before jockeying to the next cone called. This is done for several movements; then, on the call of PRESS, the player sprints forwards from their moving position, or if the call is RECOVER they turn and sprint in the direction they are not facing from their moving position.

It is important to ensure the players move within the box correctly, and if required they can perform the regression and learn the pivot action in isolation.

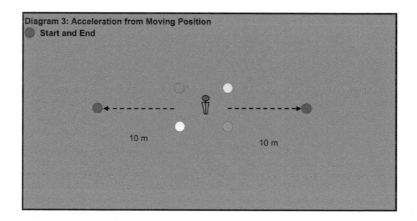

Sets: 2-4   *Reps:* 1-3

Recovery: 2-3 minutes between sets, 10-20 seconds between reps.

Progression

This exercise can be progressed so that the players are working in pairs and reacting to an opponent rather than calls, matching a game situation. In the square the player will mirror their partner: if he moves forward and to the left his partner will move back and to the right. When the player that leads decides he can sprint forward, his partner has to react and beat him over a middle line.

The drill can also be moved so that the players' squares are next to each other, and one player mirrors his opponent, until they decide to accelerate in the direction they are not facing, in an attempt to get over the ten metre line without being tagged.

These two progressions incorporate accelerating forwards and backwards from the soccer specific jockey position, as well as the reactive stimulus of an opponent that would occur in a game.

Regression

If a player is struggling to move to the cones in the jockey position, they can be taken out and taught how to pivot on the spot. Once this is mastered they can be taught how to move around the box in isolation and then moved to the drill.

Common technical errors to look for:

o   Player does not return to middle after each box movement
o   Player turns the wrong way and does not pivot
o   Player crosses legs in box

DECELERATION

Drill 1 – Closed Drill

Drill Aim – Decelerate into the Soccer Specific Jockey Position

As with the acceleration progressions, the environment in which we will progress the deceleration drill is designed to guide the players to the correct technique, but, importantly, letting them experience the right and wrong technique so that they know how the correct soccer specific deceleration feels.

This drill involves getting the players to utilise the key deceleration techniques learnt during the early phases. Begin by asking the players the advantages and then the disadvantages of decelerating into the athletic position as was done during the earlier stages. Guide them to the answer that the athletic position is not the best body position to close a player down in a soccer match as they will be caught square all the time; instead, they should adopt what is called a 'jockey' position.

The players will then perform the drill by sprinting the ten metre distance, then decelerating in the jockey position at the cone, pole or mannequin. Initially, allow the players to experiment and finish in the jockey position (i.e. half turn) on the side of their own choice; then, before the sprint, tell them which side (half turn) you would like them to finish on, highlighting to the players that if their left foot is in front they are guiding their opponent to their right side (see Fundamental Movement Skills Chapter for images).

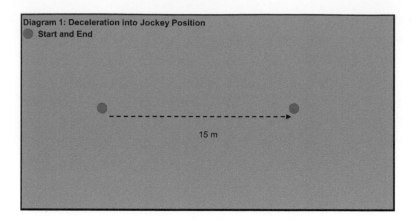

Diagram 1: Deceleration into Jockey Position
Start and End

15 m

Sets: 3-6   *Reps:* 1-3

Recovery: 2-3 minutes between sets, 10-20 seconds between reps.

Progression

To progress the drill, get the players to react to a stimulus: a call, the coach's raised arm or a ball. This will create a more soccer specific environment in which the players can practise.

Regression:

If the player is struggling to get into the jockey position they can practise this in a stationary position. Once they have grasped this position they can begin to decelerate into it. If the player is struggling to decelerate into this position, you can incorporate the cones from the earlier drills to aid with their footsteps and low body position.

Common technical errors to look for:

o   Player is positioned too side on or not side on enough
o   Player's body position is too high
o   Player does not reduce step length

Drill 2 – Closed Drill

Drill Aim – Decelerate into the Soccer Specific Jockey Position and Jockey Back

In soccer a player will decelerate into the jockey position. It is unlikely that they will then remain in that stationary position as the opposition player will react by performing an action. If this action is a pass the defending player will have to perform a sprint from the jockey position in which they find themselves. This action has been covered in the acceleration drills (Drills 1, 2 & 3). The other action an attacking player may perform is to take on the player in the jockey position and try to get round them with the ball.

To defend when an opponent is trying to take a player on, the player will have to remain in the defensively strong jockey position, whilst moving backwards. Get the players to sprint and decelerate to a cone, pole or mannequin, and then begin to move backwards in the jockey position by taking fast little steps. Utilising little steps will allow the defensive player to change their direction or their body position far more quickly than if they performed longer steps.

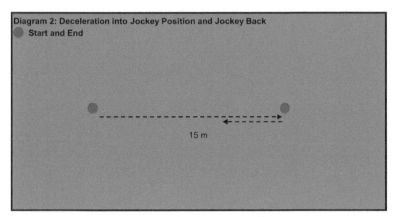

Sets: 3-6   *Reps:* 1-3
Recovery: 2-3 minutes between sets, 10-20 seconds between reps.

Progression

Once the players have mastered this and are able to move back to the start cone successfully in their jockey position, you can progress the drill by adding the pivot action to it. An attacking player will often attempt to get past the defensive player by changing the direction in which they are travelling. As a result the defensive player will have to change their body position. The best way of changing this body position is to perform a pivot on the back foot (as shown in the Fundamental Movement Skills Chapter). While the players are jockeying back a call of PIVOT should be made, whereupon the players are required to perform the pivot and continue jockeying back in this new position.

To further progress the drill, players must be told to react to a raised hand from the coach, who will be standing at the cones marking the spot where the players will decelerate. As they jockey back the coach may switch the hand which is raised and they will have to react and perform a pivot. Performing the drill in this manner ensures that the players remain facing forward throughout the drill rather than turning their heads. Turning their heads would allow the attacking player an opportunity to get past them.

Regression

If a player is struggling to perform the jockey action whilst moving backwards, they should walk through the action, gradually increasing the speed as they master the foot pattern.

If players struggle with the addition of the pivot action, they can move backwards, pivoting off their back leg each time whilst their head is maintained in the position looking forwards.

Common technical errors to look for:
o   Player is positioned too side on or not side on enough
o   Player takes large jockey steps
o   Player turns head backwards when jockeying back

Drill 3 – Open Drill

Drill Aim – Decelerate at an Opponent

Thus far we have yet to decelerate at an opponent, and within this drill we will progress the players' ability to decelerate by adding an opponent. Get the players to partner up; name one the attacker, and the other the defender. The attacking player will be given a bib to hang from the back of their shorts and told to stand at the far cone. The defensive player will then run and decelerate at the attacking player. The attacking player will then begin to jog (at light pace, roughly 50%), moving the defensive player from side to side within their channel and causing the defender to pivot. When the attacking player decides the time is right, they attempt to sprint past the defender without their bib being grabbed. The attacking player will have to perform the sprint before the five metre line, identified by the yellow cones on the diagram below.

A point is scored for the attacker if they reach the defender's start cone without losing their bib: a point is scored for the defender if they grab the bib before the attacker passes the defender's start cone.

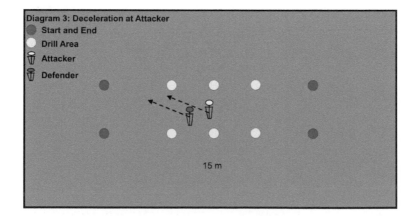

Sets: 2-3   *Reps:* 4-6 reps (half as attacker and half as defender)
Recovery: 2-3 minutes between sets, 10-20 seconds between reps.

Progression

The exercise can be progressed by having the attacker start from a moving position and accelerate from a cone an equal distance from the deceleration line as the defender, as shown in Diagram 2. This will motivate the defending player to accelerate as quickly as possible and meet the attacker as far from the defending cone as possible, thus adding intensity and soccer specificity to the drill.

Regression

If the players are struggling with the exercise, rather than working in a channel they can work along one side of it, so the defender does not need to pivot, only to turn. They can then practise pivoting while walking through the exercise as their opponent walks from side to side in the channel. Once they can successfully perform the movements, intensity can be gradually raised alongside correct technique.

Common technical errors to look for:

o   Player pivots on the wrong leg
o   Player turns the wrong way
o   Player turns and sprints before attacker sprints

AGILITY

The acceleration and deceleration drills within this phase will have developed the player's ability to start and stop. It is now important for them to combine these movement skills so that they can start, stop and move again in a soccer specific manner. As the players get older their ability to repeat these actions will be a major factor in ensuring they can physically perform at the highest level.

Drill 1 – Closed Drill

Drill Aim – Start, Stop, Turn

The first action a player may perform after accelerating then decelerating into the jockey position is a turn. This turn is defined as a recovery run within soccer, and would be used to track an attacking player who has attempted to run past them.

To perform this drill it is important for the player to combine their forward acceleration skills (Acceleration Drill 1), deceleration into jockey position (Deceleration Drill 1) and acceleration skills back (Acceleration Drill 2).

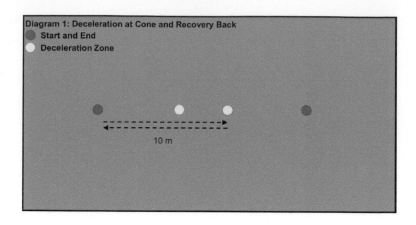

Diagram 1: Deceleration at Cone and Recovery Back
● Start and End
○ Deceleration Zone

10 m

Sets: 3-6   *Reps:* 1-3 reps
Recovery: 2-3 minutes between sets, 10-20 seconds between reps.

Progression

To progress the drill, incorporate the jockeying back action that was developed in deceleration Drill 2, and reacting to the call of RECOVER to accelerate back. This progression will make the drill even more soccer specific.

Regression

If a player is struggling to complete the different movement skills in combination, isolate the movement skills they are having particular trouble with and, starting at a slower speed, gradually build towards the full drill.

Common technical errors to look for:

o   Player turns the wrong way
o   Player stays too high when turning
o   Player does not 'whip knee' around body

Drill 2 – Closed Drill

Drill Aim – Start, Stop, Press

Another action a player would perform following accelerating and decelerating into a jockey position is to sprint forwards again; this is defined as a press within soccer.

To perform this drill it is important for the player to combine their acceleration forwards skills (Acceleration Drill 1), deceleration into jockey position (Deceleration Drill 1), then acceleration forwards skills again (Acceleration Drill 1). The player will accelerate, stopping in the jockey position, then sprinting forwards again on a call of PRESS from the coach. They should then finish in the jockey position once more. This drill can be performed in reps of two (Diagram 1), or, if the coach has the space available, they can perform several reps in a row (Diagram 2), mimicking pressing multiple opponents in a game, as they pass the ball back.

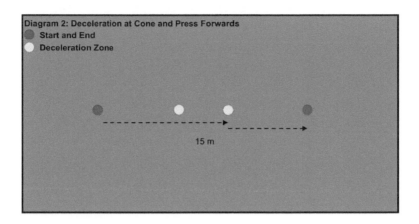

Sets: 3-6   *Reps:* 1-3 reps
Recovery: 2-3 minutes between sets, 10-20 seconds between reps.

Progression
To progress the drill the player can begin to jockey back once they have decelerated, continuing to jockey until the coach makes the call of PRESS.

Regression
If a player is struggling to complete the different movement skills in combination, isolate the movement skills they are having particular trouble with and, starting at a slower speed, gradually build towards the full drill.

Common technical errors to look for:
o   Player accelerates off the front foot
o   Player does not slow to jockey position

Drill 3 – Open Drill

Drill Aim – Agility Clock
The players will now have developed the ability to start, stop and move again. The closed nature of agility Drills 1 and 2 are an excellent environment for players to develop the correct agility movement skills. It is now important for them to perform the start, stop and move again actions within a reactive and multidirectional context, as they would within a soccer match.

This drill involves the player sprinting into the middle of a coned circle, 'the clock'. This circle has different coloured cones around the edge as shown in the diagram below. Players sprint from the start position to the middle of the clock, then sprint to the cone of whichever colour is called out. After each sprint the player returns to the start cone, and repeats the drill.

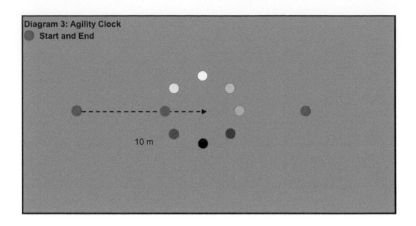

Sets: 3-6   *Reps:* 4-6 reps
Recovery: 2-3 minutes between sets, 10-20 seconds between reps.

Progression

To progress this drill, two players start at opposite red cones facing each other, racing each other to the middle of the clock and then to whichever coloured cone is called. The drill can also be progressed so that one player within the clock is an attacker and the other a defender. The defender will have to react and chase the attacker to the cone they sprint to. The attacker can be tagged, have a bib hanging from his shorts that the defender has to grab, or a reaction band (attached to both players which will disconnect when the attacker gets away).

Regression

If a player is struggling to perform the movements with the correct mechanics they can perform the drill at a lower intensity until the movements are learnt correctly. If a specific movement (e.g. backwards turn at 45 degrees) is the issue, this movement can be learnt in isolation in a closed manner. Once learnt, the player can then perform the full drill.

Common technical errors to look for:

o   Player turns wrong way
o   Player does not lower body position during transition (acceleration – deceleration – acceleration)
o   Player does not alter foot patterns

PLYOMETRIC

During the earlier phase the players will have learnt how to jump and land correctly. The next stage within this phase is to challenge these mechanics and progress them further.

To do this, equipment such as hurdles and boxes can be used, pushing the players to jump higher and still land correctly. The technique of individual players will guide the coach as to the appropriate hurdle or box height, and it is important the coach does not stray from good technique.

These progressions can also be used to further progress the player's ability to perform single leg jumps hops, over hurdles or onto small boxes.

Hurdle Jump Drills

Sets: 3-4   *Reps:* 3-4 reps
Recovery: 2-3 minutes between sets, 10-20 seconds between reps.

The player stands with feet shoulder width apart. They perform a quick dip of their hips, ensuring their bum moves back and their arms drop beside their body. They then quickly triple extend at the ankle, knee and hip, lifting their arms simultaneously, and jump over the hurdle. They land with their weight in the middle of their feet and in a quarter squat (see Fundamental Movement Skills Chapter for images). They then repeat over the remaining hurdles.

Common technical errors to look for:
o   Player raises heels when they dip for jump
o   Player lands with their heels raised and not in a correct quarter squat position
o   Player does not use their arms

Box Jump Drills

Sets: 3   *Reps:* 3 reps
Recovery: 2-3 minutes between sets, 10-20 seconds between reps.

The player utilises the same technique as they did over the hurdles but now lands on a box. The box height must be challenging but do not sacrifice good technique for height. The player must then step off the box and repeat.

Common technical errors to look for:

o   Player raises heels when they dip for jump
o   Player lands with their heels raised and not in a correct quarter squat position
o   Player does not use their arms to jump

Single Leg Hurdle Jump Drills

Sets: 1-2 (each leg)   *Reps:* 3-4 reps
Recovery: 2-3 minutes between sets, 10-20 seconds between reps.

The player begins by raising one leg and bending at the knee and hip. They then dip, moving their bum back, following this with an explosive triple extension of the ankle, knee and hip of the leg that is touching the floor. They then jump over the hurdle and land on the same leg, in a quarter squat with their toes pointing forward and knee in line with their toes. They should repeat through the remaining hurdles, and then switch legs for the next set.

Common technical errors to look for:

o   Player does not bend hip and knee when landing
o   Player's knees fall in when landing
o   Player does not use their arms when jumping

The hurdle and box jumps will not only challenge a player's jumping and landing mechanics, but also provide a plyometric exercise that will develop a quick stretch shortening cycle, which will benefit the player's ability to perform explosive actions, such as running, jumping and kicking, within a match. Learning to use the hurdles and boxes correctly is important to the player's long term physical development, as exercises with these pieces of equipment will continue throughout the older phases, and constantly develop their power.

Light medicine balls and power bags can be introduced to training, helping to develop the technique of throws and slams. These exercises will become important in building up power during later phases of the player's physical development, and using these phases to teach the correct technique will minimise the time spent on technique when the player is older. Medicine balls and power bags of a light weight (1kg–3kg) should be used, and technique should always be the coach's guide.

Medicine Ball Throw

Sets: 3   *Reps:* 3 reps
Recovery: 2-3 minutes between sets, 10-20 seconds between reps.

The player begins by holding the medicine ball at their chest. They then perform a dip at the knee and hip to a quarter squat, with their bum moving backwards. This is immediately followed by an explosive triple extension of the ankle, knee and hip, and simultaneous extension of the arms forward. This propels the player forward and they release the ball at the end of this extension.

Common technical errors to look for:
o   Player dips too low
o   Player dips and extends too slowly
o   Player does not maintain a straight body as they extend

Note: this exercise can also be performed with a power bag.

Medicine Ball Over Head Throw

Sets: 3   *Reps:* 3 reps
Recovery: 2-3 minutes between sets, 10-20 seconds between reps.

The player begins by holding the medicine ball at chest height, with their arms held out straight in front. They then perform a dip at the knee and hip to a quarter squat, with their bum moving backwards. This is immediately followed by an explosive triple extension of the ankle, knee and hip, and simultaneous extension of the arms up and over their head. The ball is released as the arms propel upwards, keeping arms straight throughout, the player is aiming to achieve height on the throw rather than distance.

Common technical errors to look for:
o   Player dips too low
o   Player dips and extends too slowly
o   Player does not triple extend fully
o   Player does not keep arms straight

Note: this exercise can also be performed with a power bag.

Sets: 3   *Reps:* 3 reps
Recovery: 2-3 minutes between sets, 10-20 seconds between reps.

The player begins by holding the medicine ball at chest height, with their arms held out straight in front. They then perform a triple extension of the ankle, knee and hip, with the ball moving over head and arms remaining straight. This is immediately followed by an explosive triple flexion of the ankle, knee and hip, the player slamming the ball down as they move into a squat. The arms remain extended throughout and the ball is released as the arms are propelled down.

Common technical errors to look for:
o   Player slams the ball down too slowly
o   Player does not triple extend fully at the top
o   Player does not maintain a straight back and finish in the correct squat position
o   Player does not keep arms straight

Note: this exercise can also be performed with a power bag.

PLANNING AND PERIODISATION

Most amateur level clubs will have just one session a week, the day before a game; this does not mean the strength and conditioning element should be omitted. It can be included in the phase topic within the players' warm up. As a result, the players will still be getting the necessary physical development without being fatigued for the match the following day. Remember, we are looking at the long term development of the young player, not the short term.

The table below shows the season's plan for strength and conditioning sessions when a coach has only one training session a week.

One Session a Week, Whole Season Plan:

Pre-season	Weeks 1-8	Weeks 9-16	Weeks 17-24	Weeks 25-32	Weeks 33-40
Recovery, Regeneration, Mobility and Stability	Acceleration, Deceleration, Agility (2 weeks each)	Gym Exercise and Jumping techniques	Acceleration, Deceleration, Agility (2 weeks each)	Gym Exercise and Jumping techniques	Acceleration, Deceleration, Agility (2 weeks each)
	Mobility and Stability exercises maintained throughout				

At higher levels of the game the number of sessions a week for the player will increase to two or three, so the inclusion of strength and conditioning can increase also. Every fourth week should continue to be a download week, where the intensity of the session is reduced, to allow for physical regeneration. Below is an example of a regular training week and what content to have when.

Example Week with Two Sessions:

Match Day	No Training	Training Day 1	No Training	Training Day 2	No Training	No Training
No S&C		Mobility, Stability, Gym Exercise and Jumping Technique		Acceleration, Deceleration, Agility		

SOCCER SPECIFIC PREPARATION

Now the players have become older there is the opportunity to introduce basic elements of soccer specific preparation into a player's training week. Introducing home recovery drills will help foster good habits, which will become more important as the players become older and require recovery from the increased match intensity.

Introducing players to activity and nutritional food diaries develops an environment in which the player begins to think about their overall lifestyle and the impact it has on their soccer performance. It is important to develop this awareness at a young age and create a fun environment in which it can be fostered. Therefore, getting players to bring in 'meals of the week' and awarding 'activity stars' for performing activity away from soccer at the appropriate times will get the players to think about their lifestyle without even realising they are consciously doing so.

AGES 14–16

The players entering the 14 – 16 age range should now have progressed successfully through the first two phases of development, having achieved an excellent level of functional competence and fundamental movement skills but also building into a more soccer specific outlook on both concepts. They should now have learnt about how to train, so this phase is where they start to train in earnest and acquire the physiological adaptation that comes from it. This physiological adaptation is enhanced as the majority of players will now have gone through PHV.

As stated, the average age for PHV in young males is 13.8 years of age, which is at the start of this phase of development. This can initially cause some problems, as immediately post-PHV the individual will experience some loss in mobility, co–ordination and body awareness. This can directly impact soccer performance, and you may find players mis-controlling and not striking the ball as cleanly as before, as their minds have to adapt to the longer limbs they now have. These co-ordination and body awareness decrements need to be worked on in closed soccer technical practices, allowing players the time to reconfigure their neural pathways; the same goes for the gym movements.

The issue of losses in mobility can be reduced by the work done in the previous phase of development at 11–13 years of age, and if maintained at home pre- and during the growth spurt. However, every individual is different and some may experience differing impacts from PHV, with a more or less aggressive growth spurt. Thus it is pivotal to take every player as an individual and tailor the plan to their needs, preparing them for the forthcoming window.

At twelve to eighteen months post-PHV there is a 'window of opportunity' for maximal gains in muscle size and strength, so it is essential that the players can capitalise on this; resulting in large gains in speed and power output. It is pivotal, therefore, that you minimise the growth spurt effects in order to achieve optimal developmental conditions during this age range.

FUNCTIONAL COMPETENCE

As mentioned above, the functional competence of players could have been affected adversely by the growth spurt so it is essential to re-affirm the earlier work. The players should regularly undertake corrective programmes at home; these should include mobility, stability and strengthening work (see Functional Competence Exercise Index). These programmes should now be more individualised for each player rather than generic, because each player will have been affected differently by the growth spurt and will require different things. In order to create these individualised programmes, players will need to be assessed.

In terms of exercise prescription, the exercises are relatively similar to those mentioned in the previous chapter and can be progressed as shown below when the player is competent to do so. The amount of reps and sets, or time, can be increased further in order to continue to progress the exercise.

	Exercise	Sets	Reps
Core	Deadbug Progression	2	8–12
	Plank Progressions	2	60–120 seconds
	Side Plank Progressions	2 each side	30–60 seconds
	Quadruped Progression	2	8–12
	Oblique Crunch	2 each side	60 seconds
Glutes	Clam Progressions	2	8–12
	Glute Bridge Progression	2	8–12
	Single Leg Glute Bridge Progression	2	8–12
	Band Walk Progression	2 each side	10 metres
	Clam taps	2 each side	60 seconds
Proprioception	Single Leg Balance Progressions	2 each side	60 seconds
Calf Mobility	Foam Roll	Each side	60–120 seconds
	Stretch 1	Each side	60–120 seconds
	Stretch 2	Each side	60–120 seconds
Hip Flexors	Foam Roll	Each side	60–120 seconds
	Stretch	Each side	60–120 seconds
	Stretch with band	Each side	60–120 seconds
	Hurdle Walk	2 each side	8–12

WEIGHT TRAINING

The goal at the start of this phase is to continue practising technique and not allow PHV to negatively impact the movements. Players who have had an aggressive growth spurt may complain of pains in joints and other areas of the body, this will limit their participation in gym sessions because they may aggravate the pain. This does not mean that these players cannot undertake the sessions but you will need to tailor them differently to give those players as much support as possible. A more corrective exercise-based approach would be a better session structure because it will allow those players to maintain functional competence and help manage the pain. In this way, when the pain eases they can get straight back into full weight training.

Session Plan for Sufferers from Osgood-Schlatter Disease

Exercise	Sets	Reps
Foam Roll – all major muscle groups	1 of each muscle group	60–120 seconds
Glute Clams	2	12
Glute Bridge	2	12
Hamstring Swiss Ball Roll Ins	2	12
Adductor Squeeze	2	20 seconds
Plank	2	30 seconds
Side Plank	2	30 seconds
Swiss Ball Squat *	2	10–12
Swiss Ball Single Leg Squat *	2	8
Single Leg RDL *	2	6

★ Only if pain free

It is important to have built up a player's understanding and functional capability by the time they reach twelve to eighteen months post-PHV in order to capitalise on the 'window of opportunity'. It is not anymore just how well the player can lift technically but also how much. However, it is still essential that good technique is maintained because we do not want injuries to occur. Even though there is a specific window to hit, as a coach you still want to have a planned progression into developing strength, speed and power, because it is a gradual process and these elements are interdependent. A generic year plan for a squad is shown below.

Year Plan:

Pre-Season	Weeks 1–8	Weeks 9–16	Weeks 17–24	Weeks 25–32	Weeks 33–40
Hypertrophy	Strength	Strength-Power Conversion	Power	Strength-Speed Conversion	Speed

The exercises themselves are not always necessarily changing; it is a question of how to plan the sessions in order to provide specificity and overload for that particular phase to gain physical adaptation. You may have a player whom you think needs to be more explosive so you want to do power work all the time with them, but that does not work in the long term. At the ages of 14–16 the important thing is to build the basis of muscle size and strength; only then will the true benefits of power training be felt. Having a periodised year plan is thus more beneficial for the players' long term development.

EXERCISE INDEX:

Hypertrophy and Strength Exercises:

Double Leg	Single Leg	Push	Pull	Core
Back Squat	Split Squat	Bench	Pull Up	Barbell Rotation
Front Squat	Lunge Variation	Incline Bench	Horizontal Row	Cable Twist
Deadlift	Single Leg RDL	Shoulder Press	Bent over Row	
RDL			Single Arm Row	

Power Exercises:

Lower Body	Upper (whole) Body	Core
Clean	Push Press	Med Ball Side Throw
Box Jump	Med Ball Push	Explosive Cable Twist
Drop Jump	Ring the Bell Explosive	Med Ball Sit Up and Throw
Med Ball Slams	Med Ball Over Head Throw	

(Strength-) Speed Exercises:

Lower Body
Snatch
Sprints (Resisted)
Jumps (Resisted)

Below are examples of four week plans from each phase. Every fourth week is a download, because you do not want to be constantly overloading the body; it needs time to recover, so a reduction in work load is prescribed. Prior to starting each session ten to fifteen minutes should be taken to warm up the body and switch on key muscles required for the session.

Example Warm Up for Week 1 of Hypertrophy Phase:
o   Foam Roll
o   Hip Mobility
o   Calf Mobility
o   Glute Activation
o   Core Activation
o   Hamstring Activation
o   Movement Prep.

Hypertrophy Phase:

Exercise	Week 1	Week 2	Week 3	Week 4
Back Squat	3 x 8	3 x 10	4 x 10	2 x 10
Split Squat	3 x 8	3 x 10	4 x 10	2 x 10
RDL	3 x 8	3 x 10	4 x 10	2 x 10
Barbell Rotations	3 x 8	3 x 10	4 x 10	2 x 10

In this phase the workload of the session is at its highest owing to the large volume of reps undertaken which are required to provide hypertrophy. The rest intervals should be two minutes. A similar upper body session can be prescribed on another day of the week with the first three exercises changed to two pull and one push exercise. A different core exercise can be used to finish.

Strength Phase:

Exercise	Week 1	Week 2	Week 3	Week 4
Back Squat	3 x 6	3 x 6	3 x 6	2 x 6
Bulgarian Split Squat	3 x 6	3 x 6	3 x 6	2 x 6
RDL	3 x 6	3 x 6	3 x 6	2 x 6
Barbell Rotations	3 x 6	3 x 6	3 x 6	2 x 6

In this phase the exercises are relatively similar to the previous phase but now with a reduction in reps so a heavier load can be lifted. The overload over the weeks is provided by increasing the weight lifted. As the weeks progress the number can be reduced further to threes or even ones to get true maximum strength. Similar exercise structure can be planned for an upper body session.

Strength-Power Conversion Phase:

Exercise	Week 1	Week 2	Week 3	Week 4
Front Squat – Box Jumps	3 x 6 – 3 x 3	3 x 4 – 3 x 3	3 x 4 – 3 x 3	2 x 4 – 2 x 3
Deadlift – Med Ball Slams	3 x 6 – 3 x 3	3 x 4 – 3 x 3	3 x 4 – 3 x 3	2 x 4 – 2 x 3
Cable Twist – Med Ball Side Throw	3 x 6 – 3 x 3	3 x 4 – 3 x 3	3 x 4 – 3 x 3	2 x 4 – 2 x 3

In this phase you would want to super set strength and power exercises, with a heavy lift followed by the explosive exercise. A similar regime can be employed with the upper body exercises (e.g Bench Press into Clap Press Up) on another day of the week. Rest intervals should now increase to at least three minutes, to allow for appropriate recovery.

Power Phase:

Exercise	Week 1	Week 2	Week 3	Week 4
Hang Clean	3 x 3	3 x 3	3 x 3	2 x 3
Box Jump	3 x 3	3 x 3	3 x 3	2 x 3
Explosive Step Up	3 x 4	3 x 4	3 x 4	2 x 4
Med Ball Side Throw	3 x 4	3 x 4	3 x 4	2 x 4

In this phase the exercises should all be performed explosively, with the box height and load in the exercises increasing over the weeks to provide overload. Reps and sets remain low so the training is with intensity rather than volume. The rest intervals should be longer (greater than three minutes) in order to allow for replenishment of energy stores. The same concept should be used in planning the upper body power sessions.

Strength – Speed Conversion Phase:

Exercise	Week 1	Week 2	Week 3	Week 4
Hang Snatch	3 x 3	3 x 3	3 x 3	2 x 3
Resisted Sprints	3 x 10 m	4 x 10 m	4 x 10 m	3 x 10 m
Resisted Jump	3 x 2 (2 without resistance)	4 x 2 (2 without resistance)	4 x 2 (2 without resistance)	3 x 2 (2 without resistance)

In this phase of training the movements you want to train are quick ones which are reduced in speed by the load; this will then enhance the speed of the movement when the load is removed. Again, the rest periods should be greater than three minutes between sets. The upper body session can involve exercises from the hypertrophy/strength index, with a weight such that a player can perform the lift at a quicker speed.

Speed Phase:

Exercise	Week 1	Week 2	Week 3	Week 4
Hang Snatch	3 x 1	4 x 1	4 x 1	2 x 1
Sprints	3 x 10 m	4 x 10 m	4 x 10 m	3 x 10 m
Jumps	3 x 1	4 x 1	4 x 1	4 x 1

In this phase the load should be lighter and the movements should be performed as quickly as possible, whilst maintaining good form. The rest between sets should be greater than three minutes. The same concept can be used when planning an upper body session; the exercises will be similar to those used in the power phase but with less weight and quicker movements.

The sessions above are only a guide. They can be manipulated to suit your own players' needs. In terms of rest periods there are obviously time frames which are optimal but when you have a squad of twenty players it is not always feasible to stick to the same time frames for all, so have players in pairs whereby one works and one rests.

You may not get the opportunity to have two gym hits in a week, so planning a session with both lower and upper body exercises is also effective and time efficient. But do not try and cram too much in: two leg exercises, two upper body exercises and a core exercise would be plentiful for a single session a week.

If you are at an amateur club and do not have the facilities or time available to undertake this level of training, you could add some body weight exercises into the warm ups. As they are body weight exercises, the reps can be increased to twelve to fifteen on exercises such as squats. But if you are performing jumps, which are a power exercise, the reps need still to remain low. Another option is to prescribe sessions for the players to do themselves; however, this is only advised if they have proper supervision from an adult who knows how the exercises should be done safely.

FUNDAMENTAL MOVEMENT SKILLS

The players within this phase should possess good overall fundamental movement skills that are specific to soccer, and you should now look to expose players to training that develops functional capacity and position specific movements.

The rapid growth experienced as a result of PHV may have detrimental effects to a player's fundamental movement skills at the start of this phase. Therefore that player may require taking a step back to the earlier phase of development drills in order to reinforce the technical points previously learnt. Once the player regains neuromuscular control of their body and the ability to move efficiently and effectively they can be exposed to the functional capacity training.

PHV is not only associated with losses in co-ordination (referred to as 'adolescent awkwardness'), but also initially has detrimental effects to speed and power. You should therefore be patient with players within the younger age groups of this phase, as any deterioration in speed and power performance will return to and exceed pre-PHV values if training is completed in the correct manner.

Functional capacity can be developed within field based sessions to complement the player's gym based programmes. These effects can be amplified during the 'window of opportunity', if the players are no longer suffering from the adverse effects of PHV.

ACCELERATION

Drill 1 – Closed Drill

Drill Aim – Resisted Sprints
Utilising the acceleration movement skills developed within the first two phases, players will now perform these with the addition of resistance. Players will perform this drill by partnering up: one individual will place the resistance band around them and the other player will apply the resistance.

Players will sprint over a distance of ten metres with the resistance applied. Before beginning the drill, at the start line the player within the resistance band will lean forward to take the slack. This will also move their centre of body weight in front of their point of contact with the floor, ensuring the force they generate with each step propels them forward.

Resistance should be applied to elicit no more than a 10% reduction in acceleration.

Sets: 3-5   *Reps:* 3-5
Recovery: 2-3 minutes between sets, 20-30 seconds between reps.

Progression

To progress the exercise, players can perform actions more specific to soccer with the resistance band (U14-U16 Agility Drills), applying the resistance for the sprint portion of the agility action.

Regression

If a player is struggling to maintain good technique as a result of the resistance band, the resistance should be reduced. Players can begin by performing lower intensity accelerations leaning into the resistance band, and slowly increasing the intensity as they start to maintain the correct technique.

No equipment alternative

An alternative to using a resistance band would be to have the players apply resistance to their partners by holding them at the hips either side.

Common technical errors to look for:

o   The player bends at the hip to break body power line
o   Poor arm and knee mechanics

Drill 2 – Closed Drill

Drill Aim – Parachute Sprints

Players will perform this drill by attaching the sprint parachute around their waist. Players will sprint over a distance of ten metres; as they begin to accelerate the parachute will apply resistance. Again, it is important to make sure that this resistance does not affect the player's running technique. Resistance should be applied to elicit no more than a 10% reduction in acceleration.

Sets: 3-5   *Reps:* 3-5
Recovery: 2-3 minutes between sets, 20-30 seconds between reps.

Progression

To progress the exercise, players can perform actions more specific to soccer with the parachute (U14-U16 Agility Drills), applying the parachute resistance for the sprint part of the agility action.

Regression

If a player is struggling to maintain good technique as a result of the parachute resistance, the resistance should be reduced. Players can begin by performing lower intensity accelerations and slowly increasing the intensity as they start to maintain the correct technique.

No equipment alternative

To apply a similar resistance without equipment, players can accelerate up a hill. The gradient of the hill should be moderate to ensure its effect on acceleration is no greater than 10%.

Common technical errors to look for:

o   Player does not remain low over first five meters, despite having parachute on
o   Poor arm and knee mechanics
o   Player bends at hip breaking body power line

Drill 3 – Closed Drill

Drill Aim – Sled Sprints

Sled sprints place the players in a strong acceleration position, with their body height low and their centre of body weight in front of their point of contact with the floor.

Players will push the sled over a distance of ten metres. Resistance should be applied to elicit no more than a 10% reduction in acceleration.

Sets: 3-5   *Reps:* 3-5
Recovery: 2-3 minutes between sets, 20-30 seconds between reps.

Progression

To progress the exercise players can increase the intensity of the drill by adding more weight to the sled.

Regression

If a player is struggling, the weight on the sled should be reduced.

No equipment alternative

An alternative to using a sled would be to have the players push a partner, replicating a ruck in rugby, the partner attempting to stop the player pushing them.

Common technical errors to look for:
o   Player bending at hip to break body power line
o   Player's step length too large

DECELERATION

Now the players should have developed an excellent understanding of how to decelerate in soccer specific conditions and should seek to develop the physical qualities which will ensure their body can decelerate when at a high velocity. The development of the ability to cope with the eccentric loading that occurs when decelerating, and the greater force put upon the body, should be worked on within the players' gym based and plyometric exercise programme. You should also further reinforce their soccer specific deceleration movement patterns within the agility drills that follow.

AGILITY

Utilising the movement patterns performed within the game, players will now develop their agility, whilst also becoming exposed to training that develops functional capacity. The drills incorporate the fundamental movements learnt in the earlier phases, within a soccer specific environment (distances and work to rest ratios).

Drill 1 – Closed Drill

Drill Aim – Central Defender Position Specific Drill
The player will perform a forward action as if to press or challenge for a ball, followed by a recovery sprint back towards the edge of the penalty area.

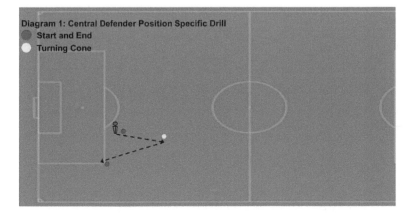

Sets: 2-3   *Reps: 6*
Recovery: 2 minutes between sets, 1 rep every 30 seconds.

Progression

To progress the drill a ball can be incorporated so that the defender presses a mannequin, performs a defender specific action (header, clearance), then chases another ball which is played in behind. The drill can also become an open drill by having the defensive player reacting to a striker whom they press and then follow in behind when they decide to sprint.

Regression

If the player is struggling to maintain a good technique, the rest between each rep can be increased: one rep every 60/90/120 seconds. Aspects of the drill performed incorrectly can be worked on in isolation.

Common technical errors to look for:

o   Turns off wrong leg
o   Turn is not tight
o   Player does not slow at mannequin, performing whole action at one pace

Drill 2 – Closed Drill

Drill Aim – Winger/Full Back Position Specific Sprint
The player will pull wide facing the play, then make a curved run down the line, 'whipping his knee' over the other when making the sprint down the line.

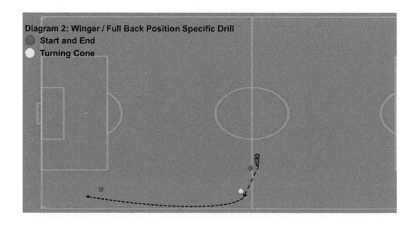

Diagram 2: Winger / Full Back Position Specific Drill
  Start and End
  Turning Cone

Sets: 2-3   *Reps: 6*
Recovery: 2 minutes between sets, 1 rep every 30 seconds.

Progression

To progress the drill a ball can be incorporated so that the player chases the ball and delivers a cross. The drill can also become an open drill by having a defender and attacker performing the drill together, the defender reacting to the attacker and trying to prevent the cross.

Regression

If the player is struggling to maintain a good technique, the rest between each rep can be increased: one rep every 60/90/120 seconds. Aspects of the drill performed incorrectly can be worked on in isolation.

Common technical errors to look for:

o   Not initiating down the line sprint with 'whip of knee' across the body
o   Player does not drop wide with small steps facing play (middle of pitch)

Drill 3 – Closed Drill

Drill Aim – Central Midfielder Position Specific Sprint

The player should perform a forward sprint into the jockey position, then press the next cone, either across (replicating a pass by the opposition between midfielders) or on the angle forwards (replicating a pass backwards by the opposition). Once in the jockey position at the second cone, they should make a sprint into the penalty area (replicating a forward run into the box if the team have regained possession and are attacking).

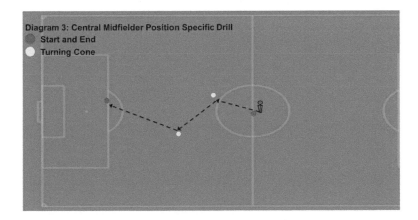

Sets: 2-3   *Reps:* 6

Recovery: 2 minutes between sets, 1 rep every 30 seconds.

Progression

To progress the drill a ball can be incorporated so that the midfielder performs a shot when they reach the penalty box. The drill can also become an open drill by making it reactive to opposition passes, the cones being replaced by players who pass the ball to a team mate when pressed.

Regression

If the player is struggling to maintain a good technique, the rest between each rep can be increased: one rep every 60/90/120 seconds. Aspects of the drill performed incorrectly can be worked on in isolation.

Common technical errors to look for:

o   Ensure player slows to jockey position when sprinting to cone and does not merely slalom through cones
o   Ensure player scans over shoulder
o   Ensure player changes direction with tight run

Drill 4 – Closed Drill

Drill Aim – Striker Position Specific Sprint
The player should perform a short curved run to represent dropping short, then perform a longer run (replicating a run in behind the defence).

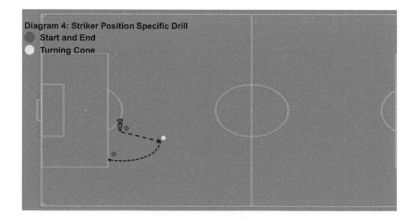

Diagram 4: Striker Position Specific Drill
Start and End
Turning Cone

Sets: 2-3   *Reps:* 6
Recovery: 2 minutes between sets, 1 rep every 30 seconds.

Progression

To progress the drill the angles the striker makes can be varied. The drill can also become an open drill by having a ball involved, the player laying the pass off and reacting to the ball played in behind.

Regression

If the player is struggling to maintain a good technique, the rest between each rep can be increased: one rep every 60/90/120 seconds. Aspects of the drill performed incorrectly can be worked on in isolation.

Common technical errors to look for:
o   Ensure initial run is curved and not straight
o   Player does not look towards middle of pitch (where ball would be played from)

The examples above can be used and developed to make more position specific drills that match the playing style of your team. Taking a high intensity movement pattern typically performed by your team and applying the sets, reps and work to rest ratio from the example drills above can transform these soccer actions into a physical development drill. Below is an example of a squad position specific sprint session.

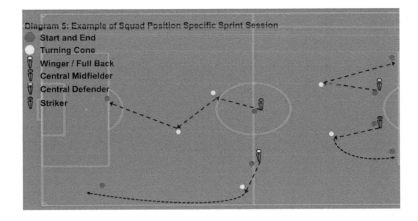

Diagram 5: Example of Squad Position Specific Sprint Session
- Start and End
- Turning Cone
- Winger / Full Back
- Central Midfielder
- Central Defender
- Striker

PLYOMETRIC

Players within this phase should have a sound understanding and technique of jumping and landing. As with the other movements during this period, some players may experience losses in technique owing to PHV. In this case, regressing to exercises from earlier phases to reinforce correct technique should be the course of action adopted. Owing to the force of impact when landing some players may experience discomfort in their knees because of the growing pains. Here, either reducing the amount of volume in their sessions or the removal of jumping and landing altogether may be required for a period of time, in order to allow the discomfort to ease.

Basic jumping and landing mechanics can be monitored and reinforced within pre-training field warm ups. However, the main focus for jumping and landing within this phase should now be to push the players to jump higher and have a quicker ground contact time, whilst maintaining excellent technique. Resistance bands can be incorporated as they were within the acceleration drills to provide overload for the body, thus requiring greater force to be exerted by the individual.

Exercises at this stage will become more advanced, with players now beginning to rebound from boxes, putting the body under greater strain and allowing greater force to be created from the resulting stretch. These exercises will be bilateral in nature and develop to unilateral in future phases. Unilateral jumps can continue to be progressed by jumping onto higher boxes, while single leg hurdle hops can be performed over higher hurdles, the contact time between each jump also being made quicker. As mentioned earlier, these exercises can be introduced to field based warm ups; if equipment is an issue, single leg bounds represent a perfect alternative. When performing high intensity plyometric drills, such as rebounds from boxes, the surface should be taken into consideration: too hard a surface, such as concrete, is a potential injury risk owing to the force placed upon the musculoskeletal system.

These exercises performed will not only challenge the jumping and landing mechanics of the player, but also incorporate a plyometric element. The exercise intensity should have increased through shorter ground contact times, which promote a shorter amortisation phase (time between the muscle stretching and contracting). Reducing the time between the stretch and contraction will allow the muscle to utilise more of the energy stored in the stretch, ultimately making the player more powerful. This ability to generate more power can then be used when the player performs powerful soccer actions, such as running, jumping and kicking, within a match.

The emphasis of the exercises is now not only technique led but also performance based, and coaches should push players to perform the correct technique with shorter ground contact times and over greater heights. Now that the players' training age has increased and their bodies are able to cope with the stresses of plyometric exercises, the contacts made within sessions can slowly be increased within this phase.

Bounds

Sets: 2-3   *Reps:* 3-4 reps (each leg)
Recovery: 2-3 minutes between sets, 10-20 seconds between reps.

The player takes a long stride forward, striking with the ball of the foot, with a quick contact time and the toes pointing up. Legs switch in the air and the player repeats with the other leg. It is important to make sure the action is springy in order to promote the use of the elastic stretch of the muscles for power production.

Common technical errors to look for:
o   The player's ground contact time is too long
o   The player's bounds are too short
o   Player does not strike the floor with the ball of their foot
o   Player does not use their arms

Resistance Jumps

Sets: 3-4   *Reps:* 3-4 reps
Recovery: 2-3 minutes between sets, 10-20 seconds between reps.

The player stands with a resistance band around their hips. A partner applies resistance and the player jumps up and forwards against the resistance. They then land in the correct quarter squat position learnt in the earlier phases.

Common technical errors to look for:
o   Player does not jump up and forwards
o   Player does not land on balls of their feet
o   Player does not use their arms

Landing off the Box

Sets: 3-4   *Reps:* 3-4 reps
Recovery: 2-3 minutes between sets, 10-20 seconds between reps.

The player stands on the edge of the box, then steps out, switching the leg that leads each rep, and landing in the correct quarter squat position learnt in earlier phases. They then step onto the box and repeat.

Common technical errors to look for:
o   Player jumps off the box and does not step
o   Player does not land in quarter squat position
o   Player does not cushion landing

Drop Jump

Sets: 3 *Reps:* 3 reps
Recovery: 2-3 minutes between sets, 10-20 seconds between reps.

The player stands on the edge of the box and steps, switching the lead leg each rep. On contact with the floor the individual springs up, maintaining straight legs (knees slightly bent). They strike the floor with the 'balls' of their feet and point their toes up towards the sky, aiming to jump as high as possible. They then land in the correct quarter squat position learnt in the earlier phases. This is an explosive exercise and if the contact time is too long the height of the box should be reduced. If available, a jump mat / opto-jump can be used to measure contact time, a contact time of less than two hundred and fifty milliseconds being the aim.

Common technical errors to look for:
o   Player is in contact with the floor too long
o   Player does not point toes up when they spring up
o   Player does not use their arms
o   Player jumps, rather than stepping, off the box

Drop Jump over Small Hurdle

Sets: 1-2   *Reps:* 3-4 reps
Recovery: 2-3 minutes between sets, 10-20 seconds between reps.

The player repeats the drop jump drill, but on contact with the floor jumps up and forwards over a hurdle. The aim is still to achieve a quick ground contact as above and the box height should be adjusted appropriately.

Common technical errors to look for:
o   Player is in contact with the floor too long
o   Player does not point toes up when they spring up
o   Player does not use their arms
o   Player jumps, rather than stepping, off the box

In the previous development phase the technical capability of using medicine balls and power bags would have been developed now the players can use these exercises to enhance their power capabilities by introducing greater loads to those same exercises. Even with greater loads they should not stray from good technique, as well as seeking to maintain the fast speed of the movement. It is important to encourage the players to be 'quick' *and* 'powerful' when performing these exercises, and push the players to perform at a higher intensity.

The following exercises can also be incorporated within power sessions to go alongside the medicine ball and power bag exercises which were taught in the earlier phase of development.

Medicine Ball Side Throw

Sets: 3   *Reps:* 3 reps
Recovery: 2-3 minutes between sets, 10-20 seconds between reps.

Standing side on with feet shoulder width apart, the player holds the medicine ball out in front of their chest. The arms are extended and the player then rotates the ball to one side. The hips remain square and the upper torso is the only part of the body to rotate. To achieve this, the player needs to activate their abdominal muscles. From this position they quickly rotate the other way, releasing the ball and slamming it against the wall or towards their partner. The action is an explosive one and the rotation back and forwards should be performed as quickly as possible.

Common technical errors to look for:
o   Player does not keep arms straight in front
o   Player does not rotate quickly
o   Player twists at the lower body

Note: this exercise can also be performed with a power bag.

Medicine Lying Chest Pass

Sets: 3   *Reps:* 3 reps
Recovery: 2-3 minutes between sets, 10-20 seconds between reps.

Lying on their back, the player holds their arms up straight above them. A partner then places the medicine ball in their hands. The player's arms move down with the ball, then quickly propels the ball back into the air, where their partner catches it. This action is an explosive one and the players should perform the transition from down to back up as quick as possible.

Common technical errors to look for:

o   Player does not push ball back up quickly enough

Note: this exercise can also be performed with a power bag.

PLANNING AND PERIODISATION

As the focus on physical development now seeks to introduce the progression of functional capacity alongside correct technique, the planning and periodisation of sessions, cycles and the season itself must be done in greater detail. Coaches will typically have greater exposure to players at these ages, and should now look to periodise the season from a physical perspective.

Resistance based sessions can also be split into separate lower and upper body days, with a typical rule of no lower body resistance work less than two days after or two days before a game. For amateur clubs that would only have one session a week which falls within this window, the coach must consider what is more important: long term development or short term success. Performing a lower volume (fewer sets and reps) of lower body exercises will still allow for long term physical development, without overly influencing the players' performance within the match.

The table below shows the season plan. The field based sessions can be incorporated into the warm ups.

Whole Season Plan (one session a week):

	Pre-season	Weeks 1-8	Weeks 9-16	Weeks 17-24	Weeks 25-32	Weeks 33-40
Field based sessions	Recovery, Regeneration, Mobility and Stability, Hypertrophy	Resisted Sprint Work	Jumps/ Plyometrics	Speed and Agility – Position Specific	Resisted Sprint Work / Jumps / Plyo Maintenance Phase	Speed and Agility Position Specific
Gym based sessions		Strength	Strength-Power Conversion	Power	Strength-Speed Conversion	Speed
		Mobility and Stability exercises maintained throughout				

The table below shows the session topics that can be performed on each day of the week, guiding the coach as to how the training week should be planned, depending on the days they have exposure to the players. Obviously, gym sessions will not be performed on five days of the week but the planner below will allow the coach to determine where they fit each of their own sessions. An amateur coach with minimal exposure to players can use the weekly session planner to provide home exercise sessions that can be performed by the players when away from training. Providing home sessions to complete away from the training session(s) can ensure the players continue to develop all physical aspects of their game, despite not having contact time with a professional.

Weekly Session Planner:

Match Day	Match Day +1	Match Day +2	Match Day -4	Match Day -3	Match Day -2	Match Day -1
No S&C	Mobility and Stability, Gym Upper Body	Mobility and Stability, Gym Upper Body	Gym Exercise Lower Body Acceleration, Deceleration, Agility	Gym Exercise Lower Body Acceleration, Deceleration, Agility	Gym Upper Body Acceleration, Deceleration, Agility	Mobility and Stability (If only session of week include phases topic in warm up)

Example Week with Three Sessions:

Match Day	No Training	Training Day 1	No Training	Training Day 2	No Training	Training Day 3
No S&C		Field Based Session in Warm Up		Field Based Session in Warm Up		Field Based Primer / Activation Session in Warm Up
		Mobility, Stability, Gym Based Session Upper Body		Mobility, Stability, Gym Based Session Lower Body		Mobility, Stability and Recovery

Training Sessions

Once players are post-PHV they can be introduced to the philosophy of getting fit through playing the game. Training drills and dimensions can be manipulated to provide different physiological adaptations. These training drills can be categorised into three different groups: Extensive Endurance, Intensive Endurance and Extensive Intervals (Verheijen, 2014).

Extensive Endurance:

Extensive Endurance training is the ability to perform long soccer actions (Verheijen, 2014). The longer rest period between actions within these drills allows for the development of the quality of these long soccer actions (e.g. 10 metre sprint followed by a shot). This can be developed through performing drills involving large sized teams, such as 11v11–8v8.

Intensive Endurance:

Intensive Endurance training is the ability to repeatedly perform these long soccer actions (Verheijen, 2014). The shorter rest durations between actions promotes the development of being able to repeatedly perform long soccer actions at a high intensity (e.g. performing two 10 m sprints in a minute). This can be developed through performing drills that involve moderate sized teams, such as 7v7–5v5.

Extensive Interval:

Extensive Interval training is the ability to perform multiple short explosive soccer actions within a short space of time (Verheijen, 2014), such as a pass every 15 seconds. This can be developed through performing soccer drills that involve small sized teams, such as 4v4 – 2v2.

These drills can be progressed appropriately throughout the season by increasing the duration of each game, the number of games, the rest period between games or the rules (Verheijen, 2014). This will create an overload session that is performed on the high intensity training day.

Examples of Progressions:

	Extensive Endurance			Intensive Endurance			Extensive Interval		
1	2 sets	8 min	2 min rest	4 sets	4 min	2 min rest	6 sets	1 min	3 min rest
2	2 sets	10 min	2 min rest	4 sets	4.5 min	2 min rest	6 sets	1 min	2.5 min rest
3	2 sets	12 min	2 min rest	4 sets	5 min	2 min rest	6 sets	1 min	2 min rest

Underload sessions involving half the duration for each rep (extensive endurance and intensive endurance sessions) or half the total number of sets (extensive interval sessions) can be performed on the moderate intensity training day of the week (Verheijen, 2014). This will provide preparation for the overload session for that theme in the following week.

Over the season these progressions can be periodised, the next progression being performed after each block.

The following planner provides an aid for the coach to plan where to place their conditioning soccer sessions within their training week. Again, as with the gym session weekly planner, only one overload and one underload soccer conditioning session will take place on regular weeks, where there are no midweek games. For the same reason as the gym sessions, overload conditioning sessions do not take place two days before or after a game. Underload sessions do not take place one day before or after a game. When a midweek game takes place no overload conditioning sessions can take place.

Training Conditioning Theme Weekly Planner:

Match Day	Match Day +1	Match Day +2	Match Day -4	Match Day -3	Match Day -2	Match Day -1
No S&C	No Conditioning Theme within Training	Underload Conditioning within Training	Overload Conditioning within Training	Overload Conditioning within Training	Underload Conditioning within Training	No Conditioning Theme within Training

Example Week with Three Sessions:

Match Day	No Training	Training Day 1	No Training	Training Day 2	No Training	Training Day 3
No S&C		Underload Conditioning within Training e.g. 5v5 4 sets 2 mins 2 mins rest between sets		Overload Conditioning Training within Training e.g. 9v9 2 sets 8 minutes 2 mins rest between sets		No Conditioning Theme within Training e.g. Match Day Preparation Tactics and Set Pieces

Below is an example of how this soccer conditioning can be periodised over a four week cycle, with a download week in week four to allow for adaptation to the physiological overload. This cycle is appropriate for players who are being introduced to conditioning through soccer for the first time.

Four Week Periodisation:

Themes	Week 1	Week 2	Week 3	Week 4
Overload	Extensive Endurance	Intensive Endurance	Extensive Interval	Download Week
Underload	Intensive Endurance	Extensive Interval	Extensive Endurance	

As a squad's physical conditioning develops the coach may adopt a six week cycle (see example below). Such a cycle allows each conditioning training category to be developed more often within a given time, whilst also allowing adaptation within each conditioning training category to develop with a two week download phase for that training category.

Example Six Week Periodisation:

Themes	Week 1	Week 2	Week 3	Week 4	Week 5	Week 6
Overload	Extensive Endurance	Extensive Endurance	Intensive Endurance	Intensive Endurance	Extensive Interval	Extensive Interval
Underload	Intensive Endurance	Intensive Endurance	Extensive Interval	Extensive Interval	Extensive Endurance	Extensive Endurance

Ultimately, it is the coach's decision how to periodise their squad's training, taking into consideration the physical characteristics of the players within their team and the time they have available to coach them.

SOCCER SPECIFIC PREPARATION

Players should now have a basic understanding of how to prepare themselves in order to perform at their peak and you should now seek to develop this further within this phase.

Depending on the severity of the growth spurt, post-PHV players will have differing mobility and stability issues, so the prescription of individualised corrective exercises to do at home is a time effective way of overcoming these functional issues. To identify any mobility and stability issues coaches should adopt functional screening tests (refer to Functional Competence Chapter).

Players should also begin to adopt pre- / post-game strategies to optimise recovery and prepare them for the next game. A home based recovery protocol instruction sheet which is provided to the players is a good way of promoting this (refer to Recovery Strategies Chapter).

CONCLUSION

Academy systems have multi-disciplinary teams which seek to develop technical, tactical and physical qualities. The examples and information given throughout the book have provided you with a plan by which you can develop the physical qualities required at the elite level of soccer in players from the ages of eight upwards. This does not guarantee you a ready-made elite player, but places them in an excellent position to obtain the coveted professional contract at the age of sixteen. It is vitally important to tailor your plans to the players you are working with, as each player will be at a different stage of development and require different advice and training to reach the same goal. Player motivation and enjoyment is also paramount for effective development. So it is essential to make sessions fun and varied as well as to build a rapport with your players in order to gain greater adherence to session outcome goals. This takes time, experience, excellent communication skills and a good standard of coaching which shows that what you are doing is actually helping those aspiring players reach their goals. We hope this book has given you the ability to develop the next generation of young soccer players.

APPENDIX

References

Bangsbo, J., Mohra, M., and Krustrupa, P. (2006). Physical and metabolic demands of training and match play in the elite football player. *Journal of Sports Science,* 24, 665-674.

Bayli, I. & Hamilton, A. (2004). *Long-term athlete development: trainability in childhood and adolescence – windows of opportunity- optimal trainability.* Victoria, Canada: National Coaching Institute British Colombia and Advanced Training and Performance Ltd.

Beachle, T.R. & Earle, R.W. (2008). *Essential of strength and conditioning.* Champaign, IL: Human Kinetics.

Beunen, G. and Malina, R. M. (2007). *Growth and Biologic Maturation: Relevance to Athletic Performance,* in The Young Athlete (eds H. Hebestreit and O. Bar-Or), Oxford, UK: Blackwell Publishing Ltd.

Bieuzen, F., Bleakley, C. M., and, Costello, J. T. (2013). Contrast water therapy and exercise induced muscle damage: a systematic review and meta-analysis. *PLoS One.* 23, 8:e62356.

Blanksby, B.A., Bloomfield, J., Ackland, T.R., Elliot, B.C. & Morton, A.R. (1994). *Athletics, growth and development in children.* Boca Raton, FL: CRC Press.

Buchheit, M. and Mendez-Villanueva, A. (2014). Effects of age, maturity and body dimensions on match running performance in highly trained under-15 soccer players. *Journal of Sports Sciences, 32,* 1271 – 1278.

Buchheit, M., Mendez-Williams, A., Horobeanu, C., Sola, A. & Di Salvo, V. (2015). Post-game recovery strategies in youth football. *Aspetar Sports Medicine Journal, 4,* 28-35.

Carling, C., Le Gall, F. & Malina, F.M. (2012). Body Size, skeletal maturity, and functional characteristics of elite academy soccer players on entry between 1992 and 2003. *Journal of Sports Science, 30,* 1683-1693.

Cook, G. (2003). *Athletic body in balance.* Champaign, IL: Human Kinetics.

Cook, G. (2011). *Movement: functional movement systems. Screening – assessment – corrective strategies.* Chichester, UK: Lotus Publishing.

Cook, G., Burton, L., Hoogenboom, B. & Voight, M. (2014a). Functional movement screening: the use of fundamental movements as an assessment of function – part 1. *International Journal of Sports Physical Therapy, 9,* 396-409.

Cook, G. Burton, L., Hoogenboom, B. & Voight, M. (2014b). Functional movement screening: the use of fundamental movements as an assessment of function – part 2. *International Journal of Sports Physical Therapy, 9,* 549 – 563.

Faigenbaum, A. D., Kraemer, W., Blimkie, C., Jeffreys, I., Micheli, L., Nitka, M., and, Rowland, T. (2009). Youth resistance training: updated position statement paper from the national strength and conditioning association. *Journal of Strength & Conditioning Research,* 23, 60-79.

Falk, B., and Mor, G. (1996). The effects of resistance and martial arts training in 6- to 8-yearold boys. *Pediatric Exercise Science,* 8, 48-56.

Figueiredo, A.J., Goncalves, C.E., Coelho e Silva, M.J. & Malina, R.M. (2009). Characteristics of youth soccer players who drop out, persist or move up. *Journal of Sports Sciences, 27,* 883-891.

Figueiredo, A.J., Coelho e Silva, M.J., Cumming, S.P. & Malina, R.M. (2010). Size and mismatch in youth soccer players 11- to 14- years old. *Pediatric Exercise Science, 22,* 596-612.

Gallahue, D.L. & Donnelly, F.C. (2007). *Developmental physical education for all children.* Urban-Champaign, IL: Human Kinetics.

Garrido, G., Webster, A. L., and, Chamorro, M. (2007). Nutritional adequacy of different menu settings in elite Spanish adolescent soccer players. *International Journal of Sport Nutrition and Exercise Metabolism*, 17, 421-432.

Hewett, T., Myer, G., and Ford, K. (2005). Reducing knee and anterior cruciate ligament injuries among female athletes. *Journal of Knee Surgery*, 18, 82–88.

Higgs, C., Bayli, I., Way, R., Cardinal, C., Norris, S. & BlueChardt, M. (2008). *Developing physical literacy: a guide for parents of children ages 0 to 12*. Vancouver, Canada: Canadian Sport Centres.

Jeffreys, I. (2012). Soccer. In: Dawes, J. & Roozen, M. ed. *Developing agility and quickness*. Champaign, IL: Human Kinetics, pp. 144-150.

Khamis, H.J. & Roche, A.F. (1995). Predicting adult stature without using skeletal age: the Khamis-Roche method. *Pediatrics, 94,* 504-507 (Erratum in: *Pediatrics, 95, 457,* 1995).

Kraemer, W. J., Fry, A. C., Frykman, P. N., Conroy, B., and Hoffman, J. (1989). Resistance training and youth. *Pediatric Exercise Science*, 1, 336-350.

Leone, M. & Comtois, A.S. (2007). Validity and reliability of self-assessment of sexual maturity in elite adolescent athletes. *The Journal of Sports Medicine and Physical Fitness, 47,* 361-365.

Lloyd, R.S. & Oliver, J.L. (2012). Long-term athletic development and its application to youth weightlifting. *Journal of Strength and Conditioning, 34,* 55-66.

Lloyd, R.S. & Oliver, J.L. (2013). *Strength and conditioning for young athletes*. Abingdon, UK: Routledge.

Malina, R.M., Pena Reyes, M.E.P., Eisenmann, J.C., Horta, L., Rodreigues, J. & Miller, R. (2000). Height, mass and skeletal maturity of elite Portuguese soccer players aged 11-16 years. *Journal of Sports Sciences, 18,* 685-693.

Malina, R.M., Bouchard, C. & Bar-Or, O. (2004). *Growth, maturation, and physical activity*. Champaign, IL: Human Kinetics.

Malina, R.M., Cumming, S.P., Kontos, A.P., Eisenmann, J.C., Ribeiro, B. & Aroso, J. (2005). Maturity-associated variation in sport-specific skills of youth soccer players aged 13-15 years. *Journal of Sports Sciences, 23,* 515-522.

Mirwald, R.L., Baxter-Jones, A.D.G., Bailey, D.A. & Beunen, G.P. (2002). An assessment of maturity from anthropometric measurements. *Medicine and Science in Sports and Exercise, 34,* 689-694.

Pearson, D.T., Naughton, G.A. & Torode, M. (2006). Predictability of physiological testing and the role of maturation in talent identification for adolescent team sports. *Journal of Science and Medicine in Sport, 9,* 277-287.

Philippaerts, R.M., Vaeyens, R., Janssens, M., Van Renterghem, B., Matthys, D., Craen, R., Bourgois, J., Vrijens, J., Beunen, G. & Malina, R.M. (2006). The relationship between peak height velocity and physical performance in youth soccer players. *Journal of Sports Sciences, 24,* 221-230.

Plisk, S. & Stone, M. (2003). Periodisation strategies. *Journal of Strength and Conditioning Research, 25,* 19-37.

Roemmich, J.N. & Rogol, A.D. (1995). Physiology of growth and development – its relationship to performance in the young athlete. *Clinics in Sports Medicine, 14,* 483-502.

Sherar, L.B., Mirwald, R.L., Baxter-Jones, A.D.G. & Thomas, M. (2005). Prediction of adult height using maturity based cumulative height velocity curves. *Journal of Pediatrics, 14,* 508-514.

Tessitore, A., Meeusen, R., Cortis, C., and, Caprancia, L. (2007). Effects of different recovery interventions on anaerobic performances following preseason soccer training. *Journal of Strength and Conditioning Research,* 21, 745-750.

Vaeyens, R., Malina, R.M., Janssens, M., Van Ranterghem, B., Bourgois, J., Vrijens, J. & Philippaerts, R.M. (2006). A Multidisciplinary selection model for youth soccer: the Ghent Youth Soccer Project. *British Journal of Sports Medicine, 40,* 928-934.

Verheijen, R. (2014). *Football periodisation*. Amsterdam, The Netherlands: World Football Academy BV.

Votteler, A. and Höner, O. (2013). The relative age effect in the German Football TID Programme: biases in motor performance diagnostics and effects on single motor abilities and skills in groups of selected players. *European Journal of Sport Science, 14,* 433 – 442.

Wickstrom, R.L. (1983). *Fundamental motor patterns*. Philadelphia, PA: Lippincott Williams and Wilkins.

Wong, P., Chamari, K., and Wisloff, U. (2010). Effects of 12 week on-field combined strength and power training on physical performance among U14 young soccer players. *Journal of Strength & Conditioning Research,* 24, 644-652.